Style Manual for Communication Studies

John Bourhis
Carey Adams
Southwest Missouri State University

Scott Titsworth
Lynn Harter
Minnesota State University Moorhead

Boston   Burr Ridge, IL   Dubuque, IA   Madison, WI   New York
San Francisco   St. Louis   Bangkok   Bogotá   Caracas   Kuala Lumpur
Lisbon   London   Madrid   Mexico City   Milan   Montreal   New Delhi
Santiago   Seoul   Singapore   Sydney   Taipei   Toronto

McGraw-Hill

A Division of The McGraw·Hill Companies

STYLE MANUAL FOR COMMUNICATION STUDIES
Published by McGraw-Hill, an imprint of The McGraw-Hill Companies, Inc. 1221 Avenue of the Americas, New York, NY, 10020. Copyright, 2002 by The McGraw-Hill Companies, Inc.

This book is printed on acid-free paper.

1 2 3 4 5 6 7 8 9 0 DOC/DOC 0 9 8 7 6 5 4 3 2 1

ISBN 0-07-250088-3

Editorial director: *Phillip A. Butcher*
Sponsoring editor: *Nanette Kauffman*
Developmental editor: *Sara Brady*
Marketing manager: *Kelly M. May*
Project manager: *Scott Scheidt*
Manager, new book production: *Melonie Salvati*
Producer, media technology: *Jessica Bodie*
Freelance design coordinator: *Pam Verros*
Typeface: *10/12 Times Roman*
Compositor: *Electronic Publishing Services, Inc., TN*
Printer: *R. R. Donnelley & Sons Company*

Library of Congress Cataloging-in-Publication Data

Style manual for communication studies / John Bourhis ... [et al.].—1st ed.
   p. cm.
   Includes index.
   ISBN 0-07-250088-3 (alk. Paper)
   1. Mass media—Authorship—Handbooks, manuals, etc. I. Bourhis, John.
P96.A68 S89 2002
808'.027—dc21

www.mhhe.com

CONTENTS

PREFACE

The goal of this manual is simple yet ambitious. The <u>Style Manual for Communication Studies</u> is designed to help reduce the number of errors made by students in their formal academic writing. It emerged out of our increasing frustration with our students' inability to communicate their thoughts and feelings effectively in written form. We might as well be speaking a foreign language when we mention <u>AP</u>, <u>APA</u>, <u>MLA</u>, or <u>Chicago Manual of Style</u>. We are convinced that either students are not receiving the instruction they need elsewhere or they forget most of what they are taught by the time they take courses in the discipline. Whatever the cause, the result is the same, most of our new graduate and undergraduate students do not know, understand and/or use the rules for writing formal academic papers.

There is an extensive body of literature in our discipline which indicates that the ability to communicate effectively in writing and orally will play a decisive role in the career success of our graduates. One of the authors can recall a student, who after receiving a failing grade on a written assignment because she had made 72 spelling, punctuation, grammatical, and format errors in a seven page paper, responded, "I don't know why this writing stuff is so important. When I graduate I'll have a secretary who will do all this stuff for me!" More recently, one of the authors served on a university-wide committee that was responsible for selecting students to receive undergraduate university scholarships. An alarming number of very bright, highly motivated students, with otherwise impressive applications did not receive support because they had made careless spelling, punctuation and grammatical errors in putting together their applications. Spelling, punctuation and grammar, as well as attention to detail and following conventions do have real world consequences.

The <u>Style Manual for Communication Studies</u> is designed to supplement whatever texts you currently use, in whatever courses you are currently taking or teaching. It contains condensed versions of the two most commonly used writing styles in our discipline (<u>MLA</u> and <u>APA</u>) and full text examples written by graduate and undergraduate students. Because the conventions have been condensed to include only those most commonly needed, students will find this style guide more accessible and less intimidating. In this case, we believe less is more. If you intend to pursue advanced work in the discipline, we encourage you to purchase the complete copies of both the <u>MLA</u> and <u>APA</u> style manuals.

This edition of the Style Manual for Communication Studies contains the following features to help new graduate and undergraduate students write formal academic papers:

- Condensed versions of the most recent editions of the Modern Language Association Handbook for Writers of Research Papers, 5th ed. (New York: MLA, 1999) and the Publication Manual of the American Psychological Association, 4th ed. (Washington: APA, 1994).
- Current examples drawn from national and regional journals, leading texts and key works in the field of Communication Studies.
- Full text examples of papers and preparation outlines written in MLA and APA-style documentation.
- Clear and concise rule boxes that highlight key conventions in both MLA and APA-style documentation.
- A revised and updated chapter devoted to critical evaluation and selection of supporting material, especially Internet based sources.

John Bourhis, Carey Adams, Scott Titsworth and Lynn Harter
September 2001

CHAPTER ONE
LOCATING SOURCES OF
COMMUNICATION RESEARCH

Many writing assignments require you to locate and read primary source material, including reports of original research, critical reviews of past research, and theoretical essays. In addition to book-length publications, most primary source material is found in scholarly journals. This chapter provides information about journals that publish communication research, indexes you can use to search for information on specific topics, and Internet resources for investigating the communication discipline.

SCHOLARLY JOURNALS IN COMMUNICATION

Scholarly journals are very different from popular magazines (such as Time or Newsweek) and trade publications (such as Advertising Age or Communication World). One important difference is that scholarly journals are read primarily by scholars and professionals, as opposed to the general public or people with only a casual interest in the subject matter. A second important characteristic of scholarly journals is that they are more specialized than most popular periodicals. Scholarly journals often are dedicated to a particular discipline (such as communication or psychology), and may even be dedicated to particular areas of a discipline (for example, health communication or nonverbal communication). Finally, popular periodicals and trade publications do not typically publish full-length reports of original research, whereas scholarly journals exist as an outlet for researchers and theorists to publish their original works.

Below are descriptions of selected scholarly journals which publish reports of original empirical and humanistic research, including their Library of Congress call numbers. (At the end of this chapter you'll find a more complete list of communication-related journals which you may want to consult in doing your research.) Note that some journals are considered "national" or "international" journals by virtue of their being published by national or international associations or having national and international circulations. Other journals are considered "regional" journals since they are published by regional associations, such as the Central States Communication Association, although many regional journals have national circulations. The journals described below are national or international unless otherwise identified.

Communication Education is published quarterly in January, April, July, and October by the National Communication Association (PN 4071 S73). Communication Education publishes scholarly articles regarding communication in instructional settings. Articles in Communication Education focus primarily on the role of communication in the instructional process and teaching communication in traditional academic environments and non-traditional settings (e.g., business, health, and legal settings). Manuscripts submitted to Communication Education must conform to the guidelines set forth in the Publication Manual of the American Psychological Association (4th ed.) and may not exceed 30 pages. Manuscripts submitted as brief reports should not exceed 14 pages. Communication Education is indexed in Communication Abstracts and Index to Journals in Communication Studies, among other indexes.

Communication Monographs is published quarterly in March, June, September and December by the National Communication Association (PN 4077 S6). Communication Monographs publishes articles dealing with communication in a wide variety of contexts, with most articles reporting original research grounded in theory. Submissions must conform to the guidelines set forth in the Publication Manual of the American Psychological Association (4th ed.) and should not exceed 30 pages (approximately 9,000 words). Communication Monographs is indexed in several sources, including Communication Abstracts, Index to Journals in Communication Studies, Psychological Abstracts, and Sociological Abstracts.

Communication Quarterly is published quarterly (Winter, Spring, Summer and Fall) by the Eastern Communication Association and thus is considered a regional journal (PN 4071 T6). Manuscripts appearing in Communication Quarterly include research reports, critical studies, state of the art reviews, and critical essays. Submissions must conform to either the Publication Manual of the American Psychological Association (4th ed.) or the MLA Style Manual (1985). Communication Quarterly is indexed in Communication Abstracts and the Index to Journals in Communication Studies.

Communication Reports is published in the Fall, Winter, Spring, and Summer (P91.3 .c66). It is a scholarly academic journal that publishes short (2500 words or less) data-based articles on a wide variety of topics related to the field of communication as broadly defined. Authors are expected to devote a significant portion of the manuscript to the reporting and analysis of research data. Manuscripts that are primarily theoretical or speculative in nature are not appropriate for this journal. Manuscripts must conform to the guidelines set forth in the Publication Manual of the American Psychological Association (4th ed.). Communication Reports is a publication of the Western National Communication Association and is therefore considered a regional journal in the field. Communication Reports is indexed in Communication Abstracts, Sociological Abstracts, PSYCHINFO, and Social Planning/Policy and Development Abstracts.

Communication Research is published bi-monthly in February, April, June, August, October, and December, by Sage Publications, Inc (P91 C56). Articles in Communication Research usually report results of empirical studies. The journal emphasizes the development and testing of communication theory that cuts across contextual boundaries (e.g., organizational communication, interpersonal communication). Manuscripts which report purely applied research without clear grounding in theory are not appropriate for this journal. Submissions to Communication Research must conform to the guidelines set forth in the Publication Manual of the American Psychological Association (4th ed.). Communication Research is indexed in a variety of sources, including, Index to Journals in Communication Studies, ERIC/EAC, Expanded Academic Index, Human Resources Abstracts, Index to Journals in Mass Communication, Psychological Abstracts, Sociological Abstracts, and Social Science Citation Index.

Communication Studies is published quarterly in the Spring, Summer, Fall and Winter by the Central States Communication Association and is considered a regional journal (PN 4071 C4). Articles published in Communication Studies reflect a diversity of topics and approaches, including rhetorical/humanistic scholarship as well as empirical research. Manuscripts must conform to the guidelines set forth in the Publication Manual of the American Psychological Association (4th ed.). Communication Studies is indexed in several sources, including Communication Abstracts and Index to Journals in Communication Studies.

Communication Theory is published quarterly and is a scholarly journal sponsored by the International Communication Association (P87 .c66x). Manuscripts in this journal are expected to address specific issues of theory development, evaluation, and criticism. As such, many articles are critical essays rather than research reports. Manuscripts must conform to the guidelines set forth in the Publication Manual of the American Psychological Association (4th ed.). Communication Theory is indexed in Communication Abstracts and Index to Journals in Communication Studies, among other indexes.

Critical Studies in Media Communication is published quarterly in March, June, September, and December by the National Communication Association (P87 C7). CSMC provides an academic forum for interpretive approaches to mass communication theory and research. Approaches represented in the journal include critical philosophy, political economy, rhetorical and media criticism, literary theory and semiotics, feminist scholarship, cultural studies, and pragmatism. Articles may report original research, critically review past research, or develop new theoretical ideas and directions. Manuscripts must conform to the guidelines set forth in the Publication Manual of the American

Psychological Association (4th ed.) and should not exceed 30 pages. CSMC is indexed in Communication Abstracts and Index to Journals in Communication Studies, among other indexes.

Health Communication is a quarterly journal devoted to the publication of scholarly research on the relationship between communication processes and health (P87 .H43x). Topics range from interpersonal (e.g., physician-patient interaction) to mass media (e.g., effects of health education campaigns) and encompass a variety of research methods and approaches. Manuscripts must conform to the guidelines set forth in the Publication Manual of the American Psychological Association (4th ed.). Health Communication is indexed in Communication Abstracts and other indexes.

Human Communication Research is published quarterly in September, December, March, and June by the International Communication Association (P91.3 H85). It is a scholarly academic journal and the majority of articles published in Human Communication Research reflect a behavioral and social scientific approach. Articles in this journal may report original research, methodological issues, critical reviews of existing research, as well as theoretical and philosophical essays on the study of communication. Manuscripts must conform to the guidelines set forth in the Publication Manual of the American Psychological Association (4th ed.). Human Communication Research is indexed in several sources, including Communication Abstracts, Index to Journals in Communication Studies, Social Sciences Citation Index, Psychological Abstracts, and Sociological Abstracts.

The **Journal of Applied Communication Research** is published in February, May, August and November (HM258 .J67). As its title suggests, this journal emphasizes the publication of articles that address relationships between actual "practice" and theories of communication, criticism, rhetoric and/or performance. Authors are expected to apply field specific "theory" in an effort to solve clearly defined social problems or clarify contemporary social issues in a wide variety of contexts. Manuscripts cannot exceed 25 pages in length and must conform to guidelines set forth in the Publication Manual of the American Psychological Association (4th ed.). The Journal of Applied Communication Research is a publication of the National Communication Association, and it is indexed in both the Index to Journals in Communication Studies and Communication Abstracts.

The **Journal of Broadcasting and Electronic Media** (PN 1991 J6)is published quarterly in February, May, August, and November by the Broadcast Education Association. As its title suggests, this journal publishes a wide variety of research in the fields of broadcasting and electronic media, including studies on media effects, audience behavior, and media technology. Contents of this journal are indexed in a number of sources, including Arts & Humanities Citation Index,

Communication Abstracts, Current Contents, Current Index to Journals in Education, Index to Journals in Communication Studies, Psychological Abstracts, and Sociological Abstracts.

The **Journal of Communication** is published quarterly by the International Communication Association (P 90 J6). Articles span a wide variety of topics, while a majority of the articles address questions related to media, culture, and policy. This journal emphasizes cross-disciplinary research. The editors recommend that manuscripts not exceed 30 pages and require that they conform to the guidelines set forth in the Publication Manual of the American Psychological Association (4th ed.). The Journal of Communication is indexed in several sources, including, Communication Abstracts, Index to Journals in Communication Studies, ERIC Current Index to Journals in Education, Film Literature Index, International Index to Television Periodicals, Psychological Abstracts, and Sociological Abstracts.

The **Quarterly Journal of Speech** is published quarterly in February, May, August, and November by the National Communication Association (PN 4071 Q3). The Quarterly Journal of Speech primarily publishes humanistic scholarship in rhetorical studies and rhetorical criticism. Submissions must conform to current guidelines of either the American Psychological Association or the Modern Language Association and should not exceed 8,000 words in length. Contents of the Quarterly Journal of Speech are indexed in Education Index, Index to Journals in Communication Studies, and Sociological Abstracts.

The Southern Communication Journal is published quarterly (Fall, Winter, Spring and Summer) by the Southern States Communication Association (PN 4071 S65). Articles from all theoretical and methodological traditions are welcome, although the journal historically has been dominated by rhetorical scholarship. Manuscripts must conform to the guidelines set forth in the Publication Manual of the American Psychological Association (4th ed.) and must not exceed 6,000 words (approximately 25 pages). The Southern Communication Journal is indexed in Communication Abstracts and the Index to Journals in Communication Studies.

Text and Performance Quarterly is published quarterly by the National Communication Association (PN2 T498). Articles in TPQ cover a broad range of communication topics relating to personal, social, and cultural performances. Authors are expected to explore performance as it relates to a variety of social phenomena. A variety of methodologies may be employed including critical, ethnographic, and rhetorical. Manuscripts must conform to the guidelines established by the Modern Language Association and should not exceed 9000 words. Articles appearing in TPQ are indexed in Communication Abstracts and Index to Journals in Communication Studies, among other indexes.

The **Western Journal of Communication** is published quarterly by the Western States Communication Association and is considered a regional journal (PN 4071 W45). The journal publishes articles in a variety of communication areas, including rhetorical criticism, interpersonal communication, philosophy of communication, organizational communication, and free speech. Manuscripts should conform to either <u>The MLA Style Manual</u> (1985) or the <u>Publication Manual of the American Psychological Association</u> (4th ed.). <u>Western Journal of Communication</u> is indexed in <u>Communication Abstracts</u> and in the <u>Index to Journals in Communication Studies</u>.

USING INDEXES TO LOCATE
SOURCES IN COMMUNICATION

Scholarly journals are indexed and abstracted in a wide variety of publications and computerized databases. Many of these resources index journals across a wide variety of disciplines. For example, <u>Social Sciences Index</u> and <u>Humanities Index</u> will help you find material from many different fields. Most communication journals are included in these broad-based indexes. In addition, there are several indexes which are devoted entirely to communication studies, and these may be particularly useful to you if you are new to reading primary resource material in communication. The two most prominent communication indexes are <u>Communication Abstracts</u> and <u>Index to Journals in Communication Studies Through 1990</u>. A detailed description of these two indexes is provided here, followed by brief descriptions of several other indexes and resources you may find useful in conducting your research.

Communication Abstracts: This index is published bi-monthly (February, April, June, August, October and December) and provides brief summaries, or abstracts, of the most recently published articles, books, and reviews related to communication, including speech communication, media, journalism, film, and other related areas. The last issue of each year contains cumulative author and subject indexes for that year. Also, issue #5 (October) includes a complete list of all publications that are abstracted in that year's volume. There are three ways to use <u>Communication Abstracts</u>:

1. Browse through the abstract entries until you find an article that appears interesting or relevant to you, then locate the article using the source citation given there.
2. Use the subject index in the back of each issue to locate abstracts of publications on specific topics, then locate the article using the source citation.
3. Use the author index in the back of each issue to locate articles by a specific researcher.

The subject and author indexes in <u>Communication Abstracts</u> are easy to use. Next to each subject or author entry appears one or more numbers. The numbers correspond with the numbered abstracts in that issue. For example, next to the topic "persuasion" you might find the numbers 251, 263, and 285. This tells you there are three sources abstracted in that issue related to persuasion. Simply locate the three abstracts by their numbers.

Each abstract contains several pieces of useful information. First, a complete bibliographic citation is provided so that you may locate the original source. Second, an abstract of approximately 150 words describes the purpose and contents of the source, including methods and results for research reports. Finally, a list of key terms by which the source is indexed is provided. For example, if one of the articles you found on persuasion was a study on the effectiveness of television commercials, key terms might include: advertising, brand recall, commercials, consumer behavior, perception, and television. You then could use these key terms to search for additional sources related to your specific topic.

Index to Journals in Communication Studies Through 1990. This index is updated every several years and is published by the National Communication Association. It is also referred to as the Matlon Index, after its editor, Ronald J. Matlon. The <u>Index to Journals in Communication Studies Through 1990</u> (<u>IJCS</u>) references nineteen journals, including, <u>Quarterly Journal of Speech</u>, <u>Communication Monographs</u>, <u>Communication Education</u>, <u>Critical Studies in Mass Communication</u>, <u>Southern Communication Journal</u>, <u>Western Journal of Speech Communication</u>, <u>Communication Studies</u>, <u>Communication Quarterly</u>, <u>Association for Communication Administration Bulletin</u>, <u>Philosophy and Rhetoric</u>, <u>Journal of Communication</u>, <u>Human Communication Research</u>, <u>Journalism Quarterly</u>, <u>Journal of Broadcasting and Electronic Media</u>, <u>Argumentation and Advocacy</u>, <u>Text and Performance Quarterly</u>, <u>Communication Research</u>, <u>Journal of Applied Communication Research</u>, and <u>Women's Studies in Communication</u>. A new expanded CD-ROM version of this index, <u>CommSearch</u>, is also now available (see below).

The <u>IJCS</u> is divided into three parts. Part I gives the title of every article in every issue of each journal from its first issue through 1990. Publication dates and volume numbers are shown for each issue. Each publication has a letter code (e.g., M = <u>Communication Monographs</u>). An identifying number is shown to the left of each article, with the publication code letter being the first character.

Part II is the Index to Contributors. For each author, articles are listed by their identifying numbers. Find the identifying number in Part I to locate the title of the article and its precise reference.

Part III is the Index of Subjects. There are six broad headings, including "Communication," "Education," "Business," and "Fine Arts." Under each heading are listings which give the identifying numbers of each article in that area. There is also a key word index of subjects that allows you to quickly locate a group of listings on a particular topic.

Here is an example of how you might use the IJCS to locate an article on deceptive communication written by Steven A. McCornack and Timothy R. Levine. If you knew the author(s), but not the exact citation, you would use Part II: Index to Contributors. Under McCornack, Steven A. (p. 542) you would find several coded entries, including M1355, M1361, and H385. Look up each of these entries in Part I: Table of Contents. M1361 would take you to the section for Communication Monographs (p. 93), where you would find the full citation for the article, "When Lovers Become Leery: The Relationship Between Suspicion and Accuracy in Detecting Deception." You would then use the bibliographic information to locate the article in the library's collection of Communication Monographs.

Suppose you did not know of any specific articles on deception, but were using the index to locate articles on the topic. Using Part III: Index to Subjects, you would look under the keyword "deception" (p. 738) and find 38 coded entries, representing 38 different articles related to deception, including M1361, which refers you back to the same article by McCornack & Levine. Unlike Communication Abstracts, the Index to Journals in Communication Studies does not provide summaries of the indexed articles. However, the great advantage of IJCS is its immediate access to every article ever published in each of the nineteen journals.

In addition to these two paper resources, there are two computerized databases devoted specifically to the communication discipline with which you should become familiar: CommSearch and ComIndex. Contained on CD-ROM and diskette, respectively, these resources are held by many libraries and also are available to individuals at reasonable prices.

CommSearch, is a CD-ROM database of 26 journals focusing on the discipline of communication. CommSearch is produced by the National Communication Association. CommSearch includes all of the information contained in the Index to Journals in Communication Studies plus several additional features. First, CommSearch includes information through 1997. Second, CommSearch allows you to search abstracts from the six NCA journals. Third, CommSearch includes the full texts for articles in the six NCA journals for 1991 through 1997, with future editions to expand to include earlier years.

ComIndex: An Electronic Index to the Literature of the Communication Discipline, is an author and title index published by the Communication Institute for Online Scholarship. It is available on diskette for IBM PC or compatible personal computers. ComIndex references 60 international journals and annuals from the field of communication. The database can be searched by authors' names or by words in article titles. Other features include the ability to narrow your search to specific years and even to specific journals. A brief description of each journal in the index also is included in this program.

Communication research is indexed in a variety of other sources, including indexes of scholarship in other disciplines related to communication. Here is a brief listing of printed and computerized indexes that you may find useful.

- Business Education Index (1940 C), indexes materials related to business.
- Business Periodicals Index (1958 C), indexes all categories of business journals.
- Communication Abstracts (1991 C), see above.
- Current Contents: Social and Behavioral Sciences (1974 C), reproduces tables of contents for 1300 journals and articles from edited books.
- Current Index to Journals in Education (1969 C), indexes contents of education journals.
- Dissertation Abstracts (1966 C), abstracts doctoral dissertations in the United States and Canada.
- ERIC (1966 C), is a CD-ROM index combining the Current Index to Journals in Education and Resources in Education. Many unpublished papers presented at academic and professional conferences are available through ERIC.
- Humanities Index (1974 C), indexes over 340 English-language periodicals in the humanities.
- Index to Journals in Communication Studies (1974, C 85, C 90), see above.
- IAC Business Index (1990 C) , indexes over 900 journals and business newspapers with citations concentrated in the field of business.
- IAC Expanded Academic Index (1990 C), indexes over 1500 journals, including many in communication as well as other social sciences and humanities.
- PAIS Bulletin (1915 C 1990), indexes books, periodicals, and documents on contemporary public issues. Continued as PAIS International in Print.
- Psychological Abstracts (1927 C), indexes and abstracts sources related to the field of psychology.
- Psyclit (1974 C), is a CD-ROM version of Psychological Abstracts.
- Resources in Education (RIE) (1966 C), indexes research in education, most of which is not published elsewhere.
- Social Sciences Index (1974 C), indexes over 350 English-language periodicals related to the social sciences.

- Sociological Abstracts (1953 C), indexes and abstracts sources related to the discipline of sociology.
- Sociofile (1974 C), is a CD-ROM version of Sociological Abstracts.

SEARCHING, SURFING, AND BROWSING: USING ON-LINE RESOURCES

Indexes are useful for locating published sources on particular topics, but there are even more timely ways of keeping up-to-date on the latest developments in various fields. A large variety of on-line bulletin boards, LISTSERV user groups, web sites, and electronic publications are available to you via computer. By accessing these sources you can "listen in" on current debates among scholars and experts, or even participate yourself! You can also locate information and resources not available anywhere in print. Below is a brief listing of several on-line sources you may find helpful and interesting. There are many more, and more are being added every day. Most sites on the world wide web also have built-in links to other related sites. Following these links is an easy way to explore sites related to your interests.

American Communication Association: The ACA is a national organization of communication scholars and professionals from across the discipline. Its web site includes extensive resources, including bibliographies, interest groups, an index of on-line books and texts, and a wide array of links to related sites. Contact the ACA web site at <http://www.americancomm.org/>

Applied and Organizational Communication Network: This is a LISTSERV discussion group with participants primarily from the fields of management and communication (app-orgcom@creighton.edu; subscribe by sending a message to majordomo@creighton.edu).

Center for Electronic Texts in the Humanities: This web site includes an inventory of electronic texts in the humanities, including more than 75 journals, and access to collections of electronic texts <http://www.ceth.rutgers.edu>

Communication Research and Theory Network (CRTNET): CRTNET is a LISTSERV discussion group maintained by the National Communication Association. Participants post notices ranging from discussions of theoretical and practical issues to announcements of conferences. Transcripts of major political speeches, such as the President's State of the Union Address or presidential campaign speeches, are also routinely posted on CRTNET. Participation in CRTNET is free. To subscribe, point your browser to <http://lists1.cac.psu.edu/cgi-bin/wa?A0=CRTNET>.

Comserve: This is an on-line service of the Communication Institute for Online Scholarship. Comserve provides access to a resource library of scholarly papers, research materials, bibliographies, syllabi, archives of online discussions, and newsletters, as well as interest group hotlines and The Electronic Journal of Communication/La Revue Electronique de Communication. Some of Comserve's services are free, while others are reserved for those who pay an individual membership fee or departments that are institutional affiliates. Two particularly useful member services are Com Abstracts, a database of abstracts in the professional literature, and Com Web Mega Search, a full text index of over 12,000 publication titles in the field of communication. For more information about Comserve, send an e-mail message to Comserve@cios.org. There is also a Comserve web site <http://www.cios.org>

International Communication Association: ICA, a major international association for academics and professionals in many areas of communication, maintains this web site. Available here are information about ICA, listings of conference programs, bibliographies, and links to other related sites <http://www.icahdq.org/>

Scholarly Journals Distributed Via the World Wide Web: This site maintained by the University of Houston Libraries provides information about on-line scholarly journals in a variety of disciplines <http://info.lib.uh.edu/wj/webjour.htm>

National Communication Association (formerly Speech Communication Association): The national office of NCA, one of the major associations for academics and professionals in the field of communication, maintains a web site that includes information about upcoming conferences, NCA members, and even job placement <http://www.natcom.org/>.

Uncover Reveal: This unique service will automatically e-mail you the table of contents of a large variety of scholarly journals. Contact Uncover Reveal by sending a Telnet message to database.carl.org and following the instructions.

A REPRESENTATIVE LIST OF SCHOLARLY COMMUNICATION JOURNALS

- American Speech
- Argument Studies Quarterly
- Association for Communication Administration Bulletin
- Broadcasting
- Business Communication Quarterly
- Cinema Journal
- Communication

- Communication and the Law
- Communication and Cognition
- Communication Education
- Communication Monographs
- Communication Quarterly
- Communication Research: An International Quarterly
- Communication Research Reports
- Communication Studies
- Communication Theory
- Communication Yearbook
- Critical Studies in Media Communication
- Educational Communication and Technology
- European Journal of Communication
- Film Comment
- Film Journal
- Health Communication Research
- Howard Journal of Communications
- Human Communication Research
- Information and Behavior
- International Journal of Advertising
- International Journal of American Linguistics
- Journal of Applied Communication Research
- Journal of Broadcasting and Electronic Media
- Journal of Business Communication
- Journal of Business and Technical Communication
- Journal of Communication
- Journal of Language and Social Interaction
- Journal of Popular Film
- Journalism Quarterly
- Journal of the University Film Association
- Language
- Language and Communication
- Language and Social Psychology
- Language and Speech
- Linguistics
- Management Communication Quarterly
- Marketing and Media Decisions
- Mass Communication Review
- Media and Methods
- Media and Values
- Media Culture and Society
- National Forensic Journal
- Philosophy and Rhetoric
- Political Communication and Persuasion
- Quarterly Journal of Speech

- Quarterly Review of Film Studies
- Rhetoric Society Quarterly
- Southern Communication Journal
- Telecommunication Journal
- Text and Performance Quarterly
- Western Journal of Speech Communication
- Women's Studies in Communication
- World Communication

CHAPTER TWO
CHOOSING SUPPORTING MATERIAL WISELY

This chapter focuses on subjective elements of effective writing and speaking. Specifically, we introduce you to the decision-making process involved in carefully selecting supporting materials for a paper or speech outline. In this chapter we identify several guidelines or "rules of thumb," for selecting and using support material. We begin with a discussion of why it is necessary to critically evaluate sources of information. Next, we identify guidelines for evaluating support material used in a speaking outline or research paper. Finally, we identify common errors related to the use of supporting material that we have encountered in student research papers, essays, and speeches.

THE ETHICAL AND PRAGMATIC NECESSITY OF SOURCE EVALUATION

Contemporary writers and speakers are faced with a double-edged sword created by the exponential growth of information. Although it is easier than ever to find supporting material, it is much more difficult to determine what supporting materials should be included in a well developed manuscript or speech. Whether you are composing a speech or writing a research report you are developing arguments using information from external sources. For that reason, supporting material may be viewed as building blocks for the author's argument. Authors must make subjective decisions concerning the use of supporting material so that their arguments make the strongest possible case for their conclusion. More specifically, writers are justified in critically evaluating sources for two reasons: First, there is a pragmatic necessity to limit the amount of supporting material included in a speech or paper. Second, there is an ethical responsibility to only include supporting material that is accurate and appropriate. We briefly expand on both of these points before turning to criteria used for evaluating sources.

Anyone using the Internet to conduct research has encountered frustration when searching for a specific source using one of the popular search engines like Webcrawler or Yahoo. These search tools return hundreds or thousands of possible sources and the researcher is left with the options of painstakingly reviewing each source, randomly checking sources that look remotely relevant, or simply giving up. Unfortunately, the researcher's difficulty does not end there. For any given topic there may be hundreds of research articles, books, government documents, and popular press articles that could also be relevant. Thus, the researcher is faced with the overwhelming task of sifting through a seemingly endless list of possible references. Because of time constraints and length limitations, one cannot possibly review and include every possible source on a given topic. For that pragmatic reason alone, careful evaluation of sources is critical.

In addition to the strong pragmatic reasons for evaluating sources, there are also compelling ethical reasons why an author must be selective about the use of supporting material. Writers and speakers alike are reminded that they have an ethical obligation to their audience. In our opinion, this is the single most important guideline that guides research. The author of a speech or manuscript acts as a gatekeeper who presents a filtered view of information to audience members and, in many cases, the audience will base their understanding of the information on what the author presents. For that reason, the author must ensure that the audience can make an informed decision about the information presented. The guidelines we present in the next section were selected because they are based, in part, on the author's ethical responsibility to the audience.

FIVE GENERAL GUIDELINES FOR EVALUATING SOURCES

When researching a topic it is often necessary to develop a screening process for supporting material. In this section we present five guidelines that speakers and writers may use to evaluate potential sources of information. We do this by presenting some general issues that should be considered when doing any research, whether it be for a speech or research paper.

IS THE SUPPORTING MATERIAL CLEAR?

Supporting material may be used for a variety of purposes in a manuscript or speech; not the least of which is to add clarity to arguments being presented. If supporting material is difficult to explain, filled with technical jargon, or requires extensive background information, it may be useless for the purpose at hand to create a clear speech or well explained paper.

IS THE SUPPORTING MATERIAL VERIFIABLE?

Recall that the primary function of correct source citation, whether it be in APA or MLA style, is to aid readers who are interested in finding additional information or verifying the sources used in the manuscript. Thus, a second guideline for evaluating the usefulness of supporting material is the extent to which the material is verifiable.

When grading various writing assignments and public speeches we have often encountered students using personal interviews with roommates, friends, and even "people on the street" as supporting material. Although these sources can, in some cases, help make topics more concrete for audience members or readers, theses sources are often difficult to verify. The same problem can occur when using personal e-mail and even WWW documents. Since web pages can be updated several times a day it may be impossible to verify what was on a particular web page when the initial research was gathered. Authors are encouraged to avoid using unverifiable supporting material when making important claims in their manuscripts or speeches. If using such evidence for anecdotal purposes, additional evidence from verifiable sources is warranted.

IS THE SOURCE OF THE SUPPORTING MATERIAL COMPETENT?

Source qualification is an often overlooked component of supporting material. Put simply, source competence assumes the source of the supporting material has some experience or expertise with the topic in question. Without such qualifications, the conclusions drawn from a source may amount to nothing more than uneducated guesswork. In public speaking the issue of source competence typically includes analysis of the following questions:

- Does the source have significant experience with the topic in question?
- Is the source considered an authority in the field?
- Has the source conducted original research on the topic?
- Is the source well respected?

For academic writing, there are additional criteria relevant to the competence of sources. Most teachers prefer that students use primary rather than secondary sources in their papers. Secondary sources are summaries of original research. For example, a textbook on interpersonal communication summarizes research on several topics related to interpersonal communication in a variety of contexts. Although the summaries of research in the interpersonal text are likely accurate and well written, they are merely re-interpretations of original research similar to an encyclopedia entry. Primary sources, on the other hand, are original published works. For example, a research article reporting the results of a qualitative research study on interpersonal deception would be considered primary. Most teachers prefer that students use secondary sources only as a way of locating primary sources. For instance, you might use the references cited in your interpersonal communication text as a starting point for finding primary sources on interpersonal deception theory.

In addition to using sources from respected academic journals, writers must also consider the credibility of individual authors on a given topic. Fortunately, writers of research papers are not required to place the same emphasis as public speakers on identifying source qualifications. Because manuscripts have bibliographies, readers can easily investigate the qualifications of particular sources if they so wish. However, the fact that a manuscript may not contain source qualifications does not absolve authors from recognizing the importance of this criterion. For any given research topic there are likely seminal books and articles that should be cited when explaining the concept. For instance, almost every literature review and scholarly article on communication apprehension cites James McCroskey's definition of the concept. Indeed, one may question the legitimacy of a manuscript that does not cite classic works in the area being addressed. By using a combination of secondary and primary sources it is relatively easy to identify key sources that should be consulted and reviewed on any particular communication topic.

IS THE SOURCE OF THE SUPPORTING MATERIAL OBJECTIVE?

Related to the competence of the source is the question of whether or not the source is biased or predisposed to take a certain position on the topic in question. Consider the current national debate regarding violence in schools. On this particular issue, a speaker should be skeptical of supporting material obtained from the National Rifle Association. Clearly, this organization and its representatives have a very strong motive for advocating a particular viewpoint on this issue.

Although bias is self-evident on a controversial topic like gun control, writers must be aware that biases can exist on any given issue: A researcher may have a bias toward a particular theoretical perspective or research methodology; a book author may have a bias toward a particular political ideology; even a friend may have a bias influencing their viewpoint on an issue. When using any source it is important to question whether individual biases cloud their judgment on an issue to such a degree that their conclusions are not sound. Moreover, authors have an ethical responsibility to point out potential biases when presenting supporting material to readers and audience members.

IS THE SUPPORTING MATERIAL RELEVANT?

The final general guideline questions whether or not supporting material is relevant to the topic in question. It seems self-evident that one should not include irrelevant supporting material. However, students often perceive an advantage to using the "shotgun" approach for researching a topic. That is, instead of focusing research efforts on key arguments, inexperienced writers often include easy-to-find supporting material that is of marginal relevance. Although this approach can give the appearance of a well documented speech or paper, careful readers and listeners can see through this tactic. As a general rule, it is wise to include a few quality sources and explain those sources well rather than including several sources that are minimally explained and have little relevance to the specific issue being addressed.

In summary, writers and speakers have an ethical responsibility to insure that the supporting material they use is accurate, objective and relevant to their topics. When choosing between various supporting material there are several guidelines you can use to assess quality. Recall that these guidelines are relevant for any project involving research whether it be a speech or research paper.

What guidelines should be used for evaluating the quality of source material used in my writing and speaking?

1. Is the supporting material clear (clarity)?
2. Is the supporting material verifiable (verifiability)?
3. Is the source of the supporting material competent (competence)?
4. Is the source of the supporting material objective (objectivity)?
5. Is the supporting material relevant (relevance)?

APPLYING EVALUATION GUIDELINES TO INTERNET SOURCES

The Internet is rapidly changing the way research is conducted. In our opinion, students are too dependent on supporting material gained from the WWW. Although the trend toward using the Internet as a primary research tool is not surprising, it is alarming. Our position is direct: many WWW sources are of poor quality and consequently are inappropriate for use in formal academic writing and effective public speaking. In addition, students are not being adequately trained to make meaningful distinctions between sources of supporting material that are credible and appropriate versus those that are deceptive, unreliable and potentially harmful to others.

As discussed earlier, the advantage offered by the WWW is often counteracted when writers do not discriminate among sources. Put simply, not all sources of information are good and effective speakers and writers must learn steps necessary for distinguishing among sources quickly. This section illustrates how several of the previously discussed guidelines may be applied to WWW sources. We pay particular attention to the issue of source credibility and qualifications and explain steps necessary for determining the source of WWW pages.

For this example we conducted an Internet search for information on interpersonal communication. Using Webcrawler, we found 720 thousand web pages relevant to the phrase "interpersonal communication." We highlight only four of the returned sites to illustrate how one might apply some of the guidelines mentioned in the previous section. These descriptions are exactly as they appeared in the search results.

IPCT-J Index Page

The Interpersonal Computing and Technology Journal (IPCT-J) is a scholarly, peer-reviewed journal, published two/four times a year. The journal's focus is on computer-mediated communication, and the pedagogical issues surrounding the use of computers and technology in educational settings. http://jan.ucc.nau.edu/~ipct-j/

Couple Communication Program

Couples learn 11 interpersonal skills for effective talking, listening, conflict resolution, and anger management. This program helps to build more satisfying relationships. http://www.couplecommunication.com/

Interpersonal Communication

Interpersonal Communication "Work by Canary and Stafford (1992) identifies five maintenance strategies (many associated with ways to manage conversations) that have proved most successful in long-term relationships: positivity, openness, assurances, networks, and sharing tasks." (Tubbs & Moss, Human Communication, p. 189) http://www.mhhe.com/socscience/speech/commcentral/mginterper...

Interpersonal Communication Articles

Interpersonal Communication articles written by a diverse group of experts, speakers, professionals, consultants, and marketing companies. The information within these articles will speed the growth of any small and home based business.
http://www.pertinent.com/pertinfo/business/communication/

Results for this search include a title for the web site and additional information including a brief description of the site, and the Internet address. Most search engines include an option to return summaries and other information with search results, however, this option may need to be selected. As one becomes more familiar with conducting research on the WWW it is easier to explore search results quickly. More importantly, experience using the WWW can help researchers become more effective at screening potential information to find the very best sources available on a topic.

Several of the strategies discussed previously in this chapter may be used to assess the quality of Internet sources. Just by examining summaries of web sites, we can quickly assess the quality of potential sources in terms of how relevant they are to the topic in question and the credibility of the source. For instance, we may quickly dismiss the second source from our example list since it is a private corporation's web page and not a scholarly source. Although it is often easy to recognize WWW pages created by private organizations, notice how the brief description of the second source leaves the impression that this web page teaches practical skills for effective interpersonal communication in romantic relationships. In fact, this source is an advertisement for a profit-making training program. For a few hundred dollars you might be able to get basic information on interpersonal communication!

Basic knowledge of Internet addresses can help you determine what type of organization created the web page and you can avoid wasting time reviewing sources like the Couple Communication Program Home Page. In general, Internet addresses follow this format:

Protocol://document-type.server.suffix/directory/file.name

The protocol and document type are typically the "http://" and "WWW" designations. The server is simply the name of the actual computer where the WWW page is located. In particular, researchers should pay attention to the suffix of the web site. Five of the most common suffixes are: .edu (education), .org (organization), .com (commercial), .gov (government), and .net (network). For our example, one of the sources came from an education server (the site titled AIPCT-J Index page), and three came from commercial servers (Couple Communication Program, Interpersonal Communication and Interpersonal Communication Articles). The Internet address may contain an additional suffix if the server is from a country other than the United States. For instance, a document housed on an Australian server has the suffix ".au" after the primary suffix.

Although this is a gross generalization, education servers and government servers may be more relevant for academic research than commercial and network servers. Organization servers may be appropriate for use if the organization is a recognizable not-for-profit organization like the American Red Cross or the National Communication Association. Researchers should understand that Internet addresses can be obtained easily, and consequently, should be used as only one potential indicator of a particular source's quality. For instance, most students and faculty can easily obtain university accounts and publish web pages with an ".edu" suffix, however, those web pages may not be reliable for academic research. In our example, the "Interpersonal Communication" site is from a commercial server, however, it is from a textbook publisher and would be of much higher quality than other commercial sites. The point is, pay attention to the type of server but do not assume that all of one type of domain is "bad" or that another is "good."

Once sites are selected for possible inclusion in a manuscript or speech, what other information might a researcher need to obtain before determining whether or not to use a particular source? Initially, authors should review each site to determine whether a source is identified, when the last time the site was updated, and what the purpose of the site is. For instance, the return address for the "Interpersonal Communication" page is for a particular file and not the main page for that web site. To find out relevant information about this site, it is necessary to scroll down to learn that the site is part of McGraw Hill's communication web site. In other cases, it may be necessary to backtrack and find the index page for a particular site to obtain this information. Once this information is obtained, the researcher can determine the credibility and biases of the source. In our example we were able to determine that the IPCT-J home page is for a scholarly journal a source very appropriate for academic writing. The other sources, however, are secondary in nature which may be fine for some speeches, but inappropriate for literature reviews and other academic writing.

Once all of this information has been reviewed, researchers should evaluate the ideas contained in a web document as if it were a journal article, book, or magazine. In particular, the researcher may apply several of the guidelines described previously. In light of the possible evidence for a particular issue, do the web pages clearly explain and illustrate the concept? Is the author, either a person or an organization, competent and bias-free? Is it possible to verify conclusions drawn by the sources? In particular, we stress the fact that information obtained via the WWW must be verifiable. Recall that verification requires that sources and arguments can be confirmed. To apply this principle, we adhere to the independent confirmation standard. The independent confirmation standard simply requires that before using any material, one should first find other sources making the same claims, observations, or drawing the same conclusions. By obtaining independent confirmation, one is fulfilling ethical responsibilities toward the audience by ensuring that information contained in a manuscript or speech is accurate. For

> The independent confirmation standard simply requires that before using any material, one should first find other sources making the same claims, observations, or drawing the same conclusions. By obtaining independent confirmation, one is fulfilling ethical responsibilities toward the audience by ensuring that information contained in a manuscript or speech is accurate.

our topic of interpersonal communication, we might seek independent confirmation by consulting volumes of Communication Monographs, Communication Yearbook, or one of the several textbooks on this issue. Effective researchers make use of a variety of different sources of supporting material, including traditional resources found in a library.

FINAL THOUGHTS ON CHOOSING
SUPPORTING MATERIAL WISELY

In this chapter we have provided several suggestions for researching and evaluating support material. Specifically, we identified five general criteria for evaluating sources and addressed the specific issue of using the Internet to conduct research stressing that many web pages are simply inappropriate to use in speeches and papers. It is wise to independently confirm any information obtained on a web page.

After reviewing this information, it should be clear that good research involves much more than simply compiling a list of sources. Good research involves systematic evaluation of sources to find the best possible supporting material for arguments being made in a manuscript or speech. We conclude our discussion of evaluating supporting material by pointing out many of the common errors we see students make in speeches and papers.

Internet addresses for web sites should not be cited as the "source" of a web site. They are addresses not sources. Instead, the author, editor, webmaster, or sponsoring organization should be cited as the "source." The Internet address is analogous to the title of a journal and therefore would only be included in the bibliography. It would be like providing the address for your school library as the "source" of supporting material found in a journal! Imagine how silly you would sound, "According to 901 South National Avenue in Springfield, Missouri . . . ."

If you cannot identify the source of the supporting material you have found on the WWW do not use it in a scholarly paper or speech. You have no way of assessing the quality of the supporting material absent this information. Try to verify the supporting material you have found from another source, either on the WWW or preferably in print, and use that source instead. If you cannot identify the source of your supporting material it is the equivalent of using an anonymous source, which is considered inappropriate for scholarly writing and speaking.

Many Internet sources are dubious in terms of quality. Before using any material obtained from the WWW, authors should independently confirm the material to ensure accuracy, preferably from a printed source available in your library.

Different types of support material accomplish different functions in a manuscript or speech. In most cases, it is necessary to use a variety of types of support material so that all of these functions are fulfilled. Avoid the temptation to rely too heavily on supporting material obtained from the WWW because it is convenient to do so. The essence of good speaking and writing is variation in source material. Just as you should not rely solely on supporting material found in newspapers, so too should you not use material found only on the WWW.

Support material should be balanced in a speech, essay, or research paper. For instance, each main point in a speech must include enough supporting material to adequately support the specific issues being addressed in the point.

WWW sources of supporting material that have printed equivalents are no better or worse than their printed equivalent. For example, The New York Times on the web is no more or less credible than The New York Times in print. The National Rifle Association's printed newsletter is no better or worse then the electronic version of the NRA's newsletter. A source that is incompetent remains incompetent whether in print or on the WWW.

We always recommend to our students to print a hard copy of any supporting material they have found on the WWW that they intend to use in a manuscript or speech. That way you have a record of where you found the supporting material that can be provided to your instructor upon request.

CHAPTER THREE
SPECIALIZED WRITING ASSIGNMENTS

In academic writing, some assignments require that you follow standard guidelines for particular types of writing. Among these are speech outlines, annotated bibliographies, research abstracts, research critiques, reviews of literature, and research reports.

COMPOSING A SPEECH OUTLINE

A speech outline is a detailed blueprint for any type of oral presentation. Speech outlines are used for any extemporaneous speaking situations including informative, persuasive, and entertainment speeches. Although the format for speech outlines vary greatly, most teachers require students to prepare a full content or preparation outline as well as a speaking outline. Full content outlines are written in complete sentence format and help the speaker plan the content of the presentation. Full content outlines include a reference page that should conform to either APA or MLA style. Although APA style guidelines traditionally require a title page, most teachers do not require a title page for a speech outline; you should check with your teacher to determine his or her preference.

The speaking outline might be a typed or hand written key-word outline that is used to help the speaker deliver the presentation. Your teacher and/or your textbook may provide specific suggestions for composing a speaking outline.

CITING SOURCES

Your preparation outline should include both internal and bibliographic references for sources used in the presentation. Internal source references are how you plan to orally introduce sources in your presentation. For example, you might refer to an article on communication research in this way: "A 1999 study conducted by a communication professor, Mike Allen from the University of Wisconsin Milwaukee, found that sexually explicit images on television . . . ." Notice that the internal source reference for an oral presentation is different from an internal citation in a written paper. In an oral presentation the emphasis is on the qualifications of the source rather than how the source can be verified (i.e., the year or title of the publication). Other techniques for presenting internal source references include:

- As explained in a February 2001 New York Times article written by Sandi Elliott, the number of ...

- The statistics included in this graph came from a report titled "Technology and Education" found on the <u>Department of Education Website</u>, accessed on March 15, 2001.
- According to the director of the Career Service Center, Dr. Cliff Schuette, who I interviewed on January 26th...
- Your full content outline should contain a bibliographic reference for each internal reference used just as if it were a research paper. The bibliographic references should be listed alphabetically and should conform to either <u>APA</u> or <u>MLA</u> style.

PREPARING THE OUTLINE

Full content outlines are typically 2 to 4 pages in length depending on the nature of the speaking situation and assignment. Your teacher may have specific requirements on the number and types of sources used in your outline. Also, most instructors require that full content outlines be written in complete sentence format and typed. You can look at a sample full content outline in Appendices F (<u>APA</u>) and G (<u>MLA</u>).

- Your outline should contain four section headings: Introduction, Body, Conclusion, and References (or Works Cited). With the exception of the references/works cited section which is arranged alphabetically you should re-number points in each section beginning with Roman numeral I.
- Beginning with Roman numeral I set on the left margin, your introduction section should list all major elements of the introduction. Typically the major elements would include the attention getter, rationale, credibility statement, and preview. Specific information included under any of these points may need to be indented and identified with capital letters. Recall that one principle of outlining is that if you divide a Roman numeral into an A you should have a corresponding B.
- The body section should outline the major points you intend to develop to support the central idea of your speech. The first main point should be identified with a flush-left Roman numeral I. Sub-points for any main points should be indented five spaces (one tab) from the left margin and identified with capital letters. Sub-sub-points should be indented ten spaces (two tabs) from the left margin and identified with regular numbers. Recall that when you sub-divide a point you must have at least two sub-points.
- Any information from external sources (including library research, Internet research, interviews, etc.) should include an internal source reference with some explanation of qualifications.
- Between the introduction and the body of the speech, between main points, and between the body and conclusion of the speech you should write transition statements. Place the transitional statements in parentheses.

- The conclusion section typically contains two elements: a summary (designated by Roman numeral I) and a closure statement/call to action (designated by Roman numeral II).
- The works cited (MLA) or reference (APA) section should not use Roman numerals or any other outlining designations, but should list the references in alphabetical order following APA or MLA style.

COMPOSING AN ANNOTATED BIBLIOGRAPHY

An annotated bibliography is a list of sources of information on a specific topic which includes a short summary of the content of each of the works listed. Your instructor may establish specific criteria for topics and work selections. Annotated bibliographies can be written using either the MLA or APA condensed style guides. Each entry in an annotated bibliography provides the reader with two essential pieces of information about the work cited: how to locate the work (source citation) and a brief summary of the contents of the book, book chapter, or journal article (abstract).

CITING SOURCES

In composing an annotated bibliography, follow the rules for citing sources of information in a works cited page (MLA) or references (APA).

THE ABSTRACT

Abstracts can be either brief or extended. Consult with your instructor for any specific instructions regarding the content of an abstract. An extended abstract provides a comprehensive but brief (100-200 word) summary of the contents of a book or article. A brief abstract capsulizes the source's content in 75-100 words. Brief and extended abstracts should be descriptive of the contents of the work cited and not evaluative. Indent the entire abstract five spaces from the left margin.

SAMPLE BRIEF ABSTRACT ENTRY

Williams, D. (1984). 2001: A Space Odyssey: A warning before its

time. Critical Studies in Mass Communication, 1, 311-322.

In this article, Williams demonstrates how Kenneth Burke's

concepts of hierarchy and the redemptive process can be used to

analyze and interpret a film rhetorically. Williams suggests that 2001:

A Space Odyssey was a warning to the human species to avoid

becoming overly dependent on technology and that the ending of the

film offered a religious vision to transcend this technological

dependence.

An extended abstract for a book or theoretical article should contain the following information:

1. a concise statement of the topic;
2. a description of the purpose, thesis, or central construct that guides the work;
3. the sources of information used in the book or article; and
4. the conclusions and implications of the book or article as suggested by the author(s).

An extended abstract for an empirical study should contain the following information:

1. a description of the purpose of the study; the research question(s) or hypothesis(es) studied;
2. a description of the subjects employed in the study including: number, type, age, sex, and selection procedures;
3. a description of how data were collected and analyzed;
4. the results of the study including significance levels where appropriate; and
5. the conclusions and implications of the research as suggested by the authors. (See Appendix C for samples of extended abstracts).

COMPOSING A RESEARCH CRITIQUE

A critique of a research article contains all the elements of an extended abstract plus a detailed criticism or evaluation of the work cited. Instructors often limit the works you may select to reports of original empirical or humanistic research in the field of Speech Communication. You may also be required to submit a photocopy of the article you have selected along with your critique. A research critique can be written using either the MLA or APA condensed style guides. See Chapter 1 for a representative list of scholarly journals which may contain reports of original empirical or humanistic research. A sample research critique is provided in Appendix D.

CITING SOURCES

In composing a research critique, follow the rules for citing sources of information in a works cited (MLA) or references page (APA).

THE CRITIQUE

A critique of a research article provides important information about an empirical or humanistic research article in two parts: (1) a summary of the article (abstract) and (2) a critique of the article. A typical research critique will average between 1,000 to 1,500 words in length. In the summary (abstract) of an original empirical or humanistic study include the following information:

1. a brief statement of the purpose and rationale of the study;
2. the research question(s) or hypothesis(es) studied;
3. a description of the subjects employed in the study including: number, type, age, sex, and selection procedures;
4. a description of the method(s) employed, including the content of surveys, questionnaires, or interviews and the procedures used to collect and analyze the data;
5. the results of the study including significance levels where appropriate; and
6. the conclusions and implications of the research as suggested by the authors.

Your instructor may provide you with specific criteria to use in evaluating original empirical or humanistic studies. An excellent resource for reading and evaluating communication research is Interpreting Communication Research: A Case Study Approach by Frey, L.R., Botan, C.H., Friedman, P.G., and Kreps, G.L. (1992, Prentice Hall). Absent specific instructions, apply the following criteria in critiquing original research:

1. **Theoretical scope**: Does the study apply to a broad domain of the communication process? How might we extend the knowledge provided by the study to other contexts?
2. **Appropriateness of methodology**: Are the study's methodology and reporting of results appropriate for answering the proposed research question(s) and/or hypothesis(es)?
3. **Validity**: Does the study satisfy the requirements for external and internal validity?
4. **External validity** is the extent to which the results of the study can be generalized beyond the conditions created by the researchers. **Internal validity** questions whether the study was internally consistent and whether or not it addressed what it claimed to address.
5. **Heuristic value**: Does the study's methodology, results, and conclusions help to generate future research? Are the conclusions non-obvious?

6. **Parsimony**: Relative to other studies, does this study provide the simplest, most logical explanation of the area being studied? Was the design of the study only as complicated as it needed to be to test the hypothesis(es) or research question(s)?

COMPOSING A REVIEW OF LITERATURE

A review of literature is a summary of previous research relative to a given topic or question. A review of literature should give the reader a clear overview of what is known about the topic, including summaries of research conclusions, various methods used to investigate the topic, and indications of what areas remain to be investigated. A review of literature differs from an annotated bibliography by providing more than separate summaries of the sources included. Reviews of literature point out common themes in existing research and draw conclusions about the "state of the art" regarding knowledge in the given area. Researchers generally conduct and write a review of literature prior to proposing a specific research project in order to determine what important questions remain to be explored and to provide a rationale for their specific study.

A review of literature is a common writing assignment, one that may serve as the culmination of a course or the first step in a larger research project like a thesis or dissertation. Your instructor may give you specific instructions regarding the length of your review of literature and the scope of sources which must be included. A review of literature might range from a paper of a few pages to a dissertation chapter of more than 100 pages. In composing a review of literature, follow the guidelines of either the MLA or APA condensed style guides, including a works cited (MLA) or references (APA) page. See Appendix E for a study that includes a review of literature.

Here is a common format for a review of literature:

1. **Introduction**: Introduce the topic and provide a preview of what is to follow in the paper.
2. **Problem Statement** (also known as Rationale): Briefly describe the significance of the research you are reviewing and/or the importance of conducting such a review. There are two basic strategies for articulating rationale. One strategy is called **negative rationale**, where you might argue that previous research has failed to address a particular area of concern. Another strategy is called **positive rationale** where you might claim there would be practical or theoretical benefits to exploring some topic in more detail. Positive rationale is generally perceived as the strongest of the two strategies.

3. **Review**: The review is more than just a string of individual abstracts. It is a thorough review organized around a specific thesis. The problem statement should provide clear focus for the review. Clear and smooth transitions between main points are especially important. The reader should be guided to a clear conclusion by the information and arguments presented in the review. In a review of literature, some sources may be treated in great detail, while others are mentioned only briefly as examples or supporting evidence.
4. **Conclusion**: Restate the thesis of your paper and summarize key points. Indicate the implications of the review, such as any new research questions, applications of existing research, or integration of diverse sources.

In his text Research Design: Qualitative and Quantitative Approaches , John Cresswell (1994) recommends designing a map, or visual rendering, of the research literature. As part of the map the writer builds a visual representation of major topics discussed in the literature as well as potential avenues for further exploration.

To illustrate how a visual map of literature facilitates writing a review, read the sample research report in Appendix E. The literature review for that report can be mapped using an inverted funnel as a visual representation. Notice how the review begins by discussing the general concept of note taking effectiveness. Next, the review explains general strategies teachers can use to improve student note taking. Finally, the literature review discusses a specific strategy, called organizational lecture cues, in terms of how that strategy could improve students' note taking. An inverted funnel is an appropriate visual representation for this literature review because it begins with general information found in literature and then presents progressively more specific information. Using such a map, or visual representation, prior to writing the literature review would help the authors of this report determine how to organize the ideas discussed in the review. Although the inverted funnel makes sense for the literature reviewed in this report, other reports might use different visual representations like concept maps or flow charts illustrating connections between specific topics.

COMPOSING A RESEARCH REPORT

A research report provides the reader with specific information about a piece of original, empirical research that the author has conducted. You are in essence reporting the design and results of your research project to a larger community. A research report follows the same general format found in journal articles reporting original empirical or humanistic research. The length of a research report will vary depending on the complexity of the study, the space devoted to reviewing past research, and to the nature of the data being reported. Research reports may be prepared following either the MLA or APA condensed style guides. An example research report is included in Appendix E. Your instructor may give you specific guidelines to follow, but most research reports follow a standard format that includes the following:

1. **a statement of the purpose of the research**, often stated in terms of a "research problem" that needs to be addressed (see previous section on composing a literature review for information on articulating problem statements and reviewing literature);
2. **a review of past research** (review of literature) relevant to the research topic, demonstrating the author's understanding of the area and building a rationale for the present study. It should be clear to the reader how your study is positioned within the concepts and theories discussed in existing literature;
3. **a statement of the study's hypothesis(es)** and/or research question(s), justified on the basis of the review of literature;
4. **a description of the methods employed in the study**: for empirical studies, a description of the study's participants, data-gathering methods/procedures, evidence of the reliability and validity of measures, and data analysis procedures; for humanistic studies, a description of the criteria used in selecting texts or events for analysis and a description of the theoretical or methodological approach taken to analyze data;
5. **a summary of the study's results**, including specific answers for each of the research question(s) and/or hypothesis(es); and
6. **a discussion of the implications of the results**, explanations for the results, limitations of the research, and suggestions for future research in the topic area.

CHAPTER FOUR
A CONDENSED MLA STYLE GUIDE

FORMATTING THE TEXT OF YOUR PAPER

TYPING

Unless otherwise instructed, all written work submitted for evaluation must be typed. The type must be clear, dark, and easily readable. Laser quality output has become the minimum acceptable standard for instructors as well as prospective employers. Use only standard typefaces such as Courier or Prestige Elite (standard typewriter faces), Helvetica or Times Roman (standard word-processing type faces) or their equivalents, and standard type sizes (ten or twelve point). Only type on one side of the paper. Never use "fancy" or unusual fonts. Do not use full justification; keep the right hand margin ragged.

PAPER

Use only heavy (twenty pound or heavier) white, 8.5 by 11 inch bond paper. Never submit any work typed on erasable or "onion skin" paper. If you use erasable paper, have a high-quality photocopy made on heavy white, 8.5 by 11 inch bond paper and submit the photocopy to your instructor. Keep the original copy for your files.

INDEX TO MLA RULE BOXES

MARGINS

Leave one-inch margins at the top, bottom, left, and right of your paper. Nothing should appear within this one-inch margin except pagination. Indent the first word of each paragraph five spaces from the left margin and set-off quotations ten spaces from the left margin. Do not indent the first word of a set-off quotation. A set-off quotation is any quotation of more than four typed lines. Do not justify the right margin.

LINE SPACING

Your paper should be double-spaced throughout, including the heading, title, text, quotations, and works cited.

TITLE PAGE

Unless otherwise instructed to provide one, MLA does not require a formal, separate title page. Instead, type your name, your instructor's name, the course name and number, and the date at the top of the first page C flush with the left margin. Note that MLA follows the (day month year) format. Type and center the title of the paper two spaces below the heading. Double-space between the title and the first line of the text of the paper. If your instructor specifically requires that you have a formal, separate title page for your paper, follow the model on the following page. If you are required to provide a formal title page, do not repeat the author, instructor, course and date information that appears on the formal title page on the first page of the text of the paper. Repeat the title of the paper and double-space to the first line of text.

```
MLA RULE BOX 1

                                                              Wagon  1

Chuck Wagon
[2 spaces]
Ms. Deborah Craig
[2 spaces]
COM 205 Interpersonal Communication
[2 spaces]
12 April 2002
[2 spaces]
              Self-Disclosure Among Dual Career Couples
              [2 spaces from title to first line of text]

   Increasingly, dual career couples have become the norm in our

society rather than the exception. Unfortunately, relatively little is known

about the communication patterns among dual-career couples.
```

```
MLA RULE BOX 2

         [start pagination ½ inch from top and right]
                                                         Wagon  2
         [space ½ inch to the first line of text on the page]

   First line of the text on the page appears ½ inch below the pagination

for the page for a total top margin of 1 inch.
```

Self-Disclosure Among Dual Career Couples

Chuck Wagon

Organizational Communication 336

Dr. Lynn Harter

12 September 2002

PAGINATION

All scholarly writing requires pagination. Number each of the pages consecutively throughout the manuscript. Place all pagination in the upper right-hand corner, ½ inch from the top and 1/2 inch from the right of the page. Include your last name preceding each page number. Do not punctuate the page number in any way. The first page of the manuscript is the page on which the text of the manuscript begins. In MLA, a formal title page is not counted as a page of the manuscript.

CITING SOURCES IN THE TEXT OF YOUR PAPER

MLA style uses parenthetical references for citing sources. Parenthetical references are placed within the text of the paper rather than at the bottom of each page (footnotes) or at the end of the paper (endnotes). The basic format for an MLA parenthetical reference is: (author's last name, followed by a space and the page(s) upon which the cited information can be found). For example:

Native English speakers tend to receive significantly higher scores

on The Speaking Proficiency English Assessment Kit (SPEAK)

than non-native English speakers (Powell 40).

As a way of adding variety to your citations, mention the author's name in the text and cite the page number parenthetically. For example:

Powell demonstrated that native English speakers tend to receive

significantly higher scores on The Speaking Proficiency English

Assessment Kit (SPEAK) than non-native English speakers (40).

When citing an entire work, the most elegant citation is to include the author (and possibly the work) in the text and omit the parenthetical reference entirely.

In Thriving on Chaos: Handbook for a Management Revolution,

Tom Peters shatters many of the conventional myths regarding

effective management.

or

Peters shatters many of the conventional myths regarding effective

management.

Follow the same rules for citing a direct quotation.

> "In general, the present findings suggest that little has changed over
> the past thirty years in the textbook treatment of communication
> apprehension" (Pelias 51).

The same rules apply when citing a source with two or three authors.

> "It is our belief and the belief of perspective employers throughout
> the United States that courses such as public speaking, listening,
> and interpersonal communication should be included as an oral
> communication core in such a blended program" (Curtis, Winsor,
> and Stephens 13).

When citing a work with more than three authors, name the first author and
include the abbreviation "et al." (meaning "and others") followed by a space
and page number(s).

> "Authority, personal experience, intuition, custom, and magic may
> be good starting points for the systematic pursuit of knowledge, but
> they don't necessarily lead to valid knowledge about the world"
> (Frey et al. 6).

When a direct quotation exceeds four typed lines in length, <u>MLA</u> requires that
the quotation be "set-off" from the rest of the text. Introduce and cite the
quotation as you would normally, omit the quotation marks, indent the entire
quotation ten spaces from the left margin, and write it in block form within the
text. For example:

> This particular study raises a number of issues that have heuristic
> value.
>> The anxiety actually experienced during the communication
>> event was not thought to affect the CA trait. In fact, reducing CA
>> was discussed in terms of clinical treatment such as systematic

desensitization. The results of the present study indicate that

communication state anxiety experiences could reduce trait CA.

(McCroskey et al. 181-2)

MLA RULE BOX 3

In MLA the correct punctuation for a block quotation goes at the end of the last word of the quotation, not at the end of the citation. Do not include any punctuation at the end of the citation.

Note that the appropriate punctuation for a block quotation goes at the end of the last word of the quotation, not at the end of the citation. Do not include any punctuation at the end of the citation.

When citing a single work by an author of two or more works in the text of your paper, include the author's last name followed by a comma and the complete title (if relatively short) or an abbreviated version of the full title (if relatively long).

All groups develop fluid status hierarchies over time (Bourhis,

"Status in Small Groups"). The gradual development of these status

hierarchies have a profound effect upon role development (Bourhis,

"Role Development in Small Groups") as well as the formation of

normative behavior (Bourhis, "Norms").

CITING SOURCES OBTAINED ELECTRONICALLY

Increasingly, students and faculty are making use of electronic sources of information when conducting research. The days of card catalogs and wandering aimlessly through dusty library shelves looking for sources of information are over. Even the phrase "card catalog" may be meaningless for many contemporary writers. Current editions of the Modern Language Association and the American Psychological Association manuals do not include conventions for citing information obtained via the four most commonly used sources of electronic information: WWW pages, electronic collections, discussion lists, and electronic mail. Fortunately, suggested conventions for citing these forms of electronic material are available on-line. In particular, we suggest that you consult the MLA home page for updated conventions for all forms of citations, including electronic materials:

The goal of any form of citation is to allow the information you have used in your manuscript to be retrieved again; either by you or someone else interested in your topic. Your citation must be complete and must allow someone else to retrace your steps in obtaining the information electronically. With electronic citations, it is especially important that punctuation and capitalization be accurate in the address. Use standard MLA rules and conventions for citing authors and sources discussed previously in this section, including rules for capitalization. The MLA home page provides the following guidelines for citing electronic material:

- Identify the name of the author, editor, compiler, or translator of the source (if available), reversed for alphabetizing and followed by any appropriate abbreviations (e.g., Ed.).
- Identify the title of the work whether it be a speech, poem, or article. If it is a posting from a discussion list, provide the title from the subject line in quotation marks followed by the descriptor online posting. If the source is a web page, underline the title of the page or indicate some descriptor like Home Page if no title is provided.
- Provide the date of publication or of the last update if available. For discussion group postings or electronic mail, indicate the date of the message.
- Name the institution, sponsoring organization, or discussion group responsible for producing the source.
- Indicate the date that the material was accessed by the researcher.
- Provide a complete electronic address or URL of the source in angle brackets.

MLA RULE BOX 4

When must I document a source?
You must document a source whenever you:
  1. directly quote, word-for-word, someone else's work;
  2. paraphrase or summarize someone else's work; and
  3. use facts and data that are not common knowledge.
As a general rule, when in doubt, provide a citation. You will rarely be penalized by your instructor for giving credit to someone's work.

In general, these guidelines require electronic sources to follow the following format that can readily be adapted to various forms of electronic material:

Author's last name, first name. "Title of Specific Article, Web
File, or Online Posting." Underline the Web Site Title or use a
descriptor like Online Posting. Date of Publication or Revision.
Name of Sponsoring Institution. Date Accessed <Complete
Electronic Address>.

PRIMARY VERSUS SECONDARY SOURCE MATERIAL

To properly evaluate sources, you need to determine whether or not your
supporting material is from a primary or secondary source. Primary source
material (direct) is the raw data, information or opinion of an author. Secondary
source material (indirect) is raw data, information or opinion that has been
summarized by someone other than the original creator. If someone conducts a
study that examines the relationship between communication apprehension and
academic achievement and publishes the results of the study, that author is a
primary source. If another author quotes the original article and you read that
quotation, you are reading a secondary source. For example, when citing a
textbook you are often relying on a secondary source, the author of the textbook
who is summarizing work done by others. You are trusting that the author of the
text has read and analyzed primary source material and is accurately and
objectively summarizing that material in the text.

MLA RULE BOX 5

As a general rule it is always preferable to rely on primary versus
secondary source material in your writing. Reliance on primary source
material results in scholarship that is more credible and persuasive. For
this reason, graduate students may be required to use only primary
source material in their scholarly writing, particularly for the thesis and
dissertation.

CITING A SECONDARY SOURCE IN YOUR MANUSCRIPT

To document to the reader that you are relying upon secondary source material
in your manuscript, use the abbreviation "qtd. in" ("quoted in") in your in text
citation. In the list of works cited, only include the source you consulted
(secondary source), not the primary source you are citing.

Celia Green once wrote that ,"The way to do research is to attack the facts at the point of greatest astonishment" (qtd. in Reinhard 183).

In this example Celia Green is the primary source and John Reinhard is the secondary source. In the list of works cited the citation would read:

Works Cited

Reinhard, John. Introduction to Communication Research. 3rd ed.
    Boston: McGraw-Hill, 2001.

INDEX TO MLA WORKS CITED ENTRIES

BOOKS
1. One author, 43
2. Two authors, 43
3. Three or more authors, 43
4. Two or more works by the same author, 44
5. Book with an editor, 44
6. Book with two editors, 44
7. An edition other than the first, 44
8. A work in a book, 44
9. A translation, 45

ARTICLES
10. One author, 45
11. Two or three authors, 46
12. Four or more authors, 46
13. Monthly or bimonthly periodical, 46
14. Weekly or biweekly periodical, 46

NEWSPAPERS
15. Signed article from a daily newspaper, 46
16. Unsigned article from a daily newspaper, 47
17. Signed editorial from a daily newspaper, 47
18. Unsigned editorial from a daily newspaper, 47

MANUSCRIPTS
19. Unpublished manuscript, 47
20. Manuscript presented at a conference, 47

PERSONAL INTERVIEWS
21. Personal interview, 47

PUBLIC LECTURE
22. Public lecture, 48
23. Two or more lectures by the same speaker, 48

FILM
24. Films, 48

TELEVISION PROGRAM
25. Television program, 49

RADIO BROADCAST
26. Radio Broadcasts, 49

ENCYCLOPEDIA OR DICTIONARY
27. Encyclopedia or dictionary, 49

ELECTRONIC SOURCES
28. World Wide Web, 49
29. Electronic Collection, 50
30. Discussion List, 50
31. Electronic Mail, 50
32. Article in an online publication, 50
33. Online book, 51

SAMPLE <u>MLA</u> ENTRIES

BOOKS

The basic format for a book entry includes: author's name; title of part of book; title of the book; editor, translator, or compiler; edition; place of publication; publisher; and date of publication.

1. BOOK WITH ONE AUTHOR

Northouse, Peter. <u>Leadership: Theory and Practice</u>. Thousand Oaks: SAGE

Publications, 1997.

Kanter, Rosabeth. <u>Men and Women of the Corporation</u>. New York: Basic

Books, 1977.

2. BOOK WITH TWO AUTHORS

Kotter, John and James Heskett. <u>Corporate Culture and Performance</u>. New

York: The Free Press, 1992.

MLA RULE BOX 6

How do I know which words to capitalize in the title of a book?

In book titles and subtitles, capitalize the first word, the last word and all principle words. Capitalize all nouns, pronouns, adjectives and adverbs. Do not capitalize coordinating conjunctions (e.g., and, but, for, nor, or) or prepositions introducing phrases (e.g., of, before, in, to). Do not capitalize an article (e.g., a, an, the) unless it is the first word in a title. Separate titles from subtitles with a colon and capitalize the first word after the colon. Include any other punctuation that is part of the title.

---

3. BOOK WITH THREE AUTHORS

Brilhart, John et al. <u>Practical Public Speaking</u>. New York: HarperCollins

Publishers, 1993.

Frey, Lawrence et al. <u>Investigating Communication: An Introduction to
Research Methods</u>. Englewood Cliffs: Prentice Hall, 1991.

4. TWO OR MORE BOOKS BY THE SAME AUTHOR

Bales, Robert. <u>Interaction Process Analysis: A Method for the Study of Small
Groups</u>. Reading: Addison-Wesley Publishing Company, 1950.

—. <u>Personality and Interpersonal Behavior</u>. New York: Holt, Rinehart and
Winston, 1970.

5. BOOK WITH AN EDITOR

Collins, Randall, Ed. <u>Three Sociological Traditions: Selected Readings</u>.
New York: Oxford University Press, 1985.

6. BOOK WITH TWO EDITORS

Knapp, Mark, and Gerald Miller, Eds. <u>Handbook of Interpersonal
Communication</u>. Beverly Hills: Sage Publications, 1985.

Putnam, Linda, and Michael Pacanowsky, Eds. <u>Communication and
Organizations: An Interpretive Approach</u>. Beverly Hills: Sage
Publications, 1983.

7. AN EDITION OTHER THAN THE FIRST

Babbie, Earl. <u>Survey Research Methods</u>. 2nd ed. Belmont: Wadsworth
Publishing Company, 1997.

Vogt, Paul. <u>Dictionary of Statistics and Methodology: A Nontechnical Guide
for the Social Sciences</u>. 2nd ed. Thousand Oaks: SAGE Publications, 1999.

8. A WORK IN A BOOK

Redding, Charles. "Stumbling Toward Identity: The Emergence of
Organizational Communication as a Field of Study." <u>Organizational
Communication: Traditional Themes and New Directions</u>. Eds. Robert
McPhee and Phillip Tompkins. Beverly Hills: Sage Publications, 1985. 15-54.

MLA RULE BOX 7

The page numbers at the end of the citation indicate the first and last pages of the work in a book. Type two-digit page numbers as they appear in the book. If the first two digits of three-digit page numbers are identical, delete the first digit of the second page number (e.g., 201-02).

---

9. A TRANSLATION

Aristotle. The Rhetoric. Trans. W. Rys Roberts. New York: Modern Library,

1954.

Cicero. Rhetorica ad Herennium. Trans. Harry Caplan. Cambridge: Harvard

University Press, 1954.

ARTICLES

The basic format for an article entry includes: author's name; title of article; name of periodical; volume number; date of publication; and page numbers. The page numbers at the end of the citation indicate the first and last pages of the article. Type two-digit page numbers as they appear in the article. If the first two digits of three-digit page numbers are identical, delete the first digit of the second page number (201-02). If the first two digits of four digit page numbers are identical, delete the first two digits of the second page number (1112-13).

10. ARTICLE WITH ONE AUTHOR

Asker, Barry. "Student Reticence and Oral Testing: A Hong Kong Study of

Willingness to Communicate." Communication Research Reports 15 (1999):

162-168.

MLA RULE BOX 8

How do I know which words to capitalize in article and journal titles?

Follow the rules for capitalizing words in book titles.

---

11. ARTICLE WITH TWO OR THREE AUTHORS

Ayres, Joe and Brian Heuett. "The Relationship Between Visual Imagery and

Public Speaking Apprehension." Communication Reports 40 (1997): 87-94.

Kramer, Michael, Ronda Callister, and Daniel Turban. "Information-Receiving

and Information-Giving During Job Transitions." Western Journal of

Communication 59 (1995): 151-170.

12. ARTICLE WITH FOUR OR MORE AUTHORS

Buller, David et al. "Interpersonal Deception: I. Deceivers' Reactions to

Receivers' Suspicions and Probing." Communication Monographs

58 (1991): 1-24.

Kreps, Gary et al. "Applied Communication Research: Scholarship That Can

Make a Difference." Applied Communication Research 19 (1991): 71-87.

13. ARTICLE IN A MONTHLY OR BIMONTHLY PERIODICAL

Erbe, Bonnie. "Madame President?" Working Woman June 1999: 24.

14. ARTICLE IN A WEEKLY OR BIWEEKLY PERIODICAL

Cloud, John. "Just a Routine School Shooting." Time 15 (31 May1999): 34-43.

NEWSPAPERS

The basic format for a newspaper entry includes: author's name; article title;
name of newspaper; date; and page.

15. SIGNED ARTICLE FROM A DAILY NEWSPAPER

Gordon, Michael. "Spy Plane Episode Sharpens Debate Over Taiwan Arms."

The New York Times. 15 April 2001: 1.

```
┌─────────────────────────────────────────────────────────────┐
│                      MLA RULE BOX  9                          │
│                                                               │
│  When citing an article in a journal or periodical, when do I use │
│  quotation marks and when do I underline?                     │
│                                                               │
│  Place the full title of an article in quotation marks. Put the appropriate │
│  concluding punctuation before the closing quotation mark. Underline │
│  the name of the periodical or journal.                       │
└─────────────────────────────────────────────────────────────┘
```

16. UNSIGNED ARTICLE FROM A DAILY NEWSPAPER

"Surprise: More Nuclear Families." The Christian Science Monitor 13 April

2001: 1.

17. SIGNED EDITORIAL FROM A DAILY NEWSPAPER

Gong, Gerrit. "Lessons from the China Standoff." The Christian Science

Monitor. 13 April 2001: 11.

18. UNSIGNED EDITORIAL FROM A DAILY NEWSPAPER

"It's Time for Greens to go Nuclear." The Wall Street Journal 17 April 2001:

A20.

MANUSCRIPTS

19. UNPUBLISHED MANUSCRIPT

Borich, Lynn. "Classrooms Without Walls: The Future of Internet-based

Instruction." Unpublished manuscript, 1999.

20. UNPUBLISHED PAPER PRESENTED AT PROFESSIONAL MEETING

Stewart, Charles and Carey Adams. "Communication Style, Leader-member

Exchange, and Communication Satisfaction." National Communication

Association, Nov., 1997, Chicago

21. PERSONAL INTERVIEWS

The basic format for a personal interview includes: interviewees' name; the kind
of interview conducted (Personal interview or Telephone interview); and date.

Einhellig, Frank. Telephone interview. 25 Jan. 2002.

Dillon, Randy, and Gloria Galanes. Personal interview. 1 Feb. 2002.

22. LECTURES

The basic format for a lecture includes: lecturer's name; title of lecture; the sponsoring organization or meeting; place where lecture was delivered; and date. If there is no title use an appropriate descriptive label (Lecture, Address, Speech, Presentation).

Allen, Mike. "Statistics for Dummies." University of Wisconsin at Milwaukee, Milwaukee. 1 Sept. 2002.

Kyly, Jerri Lynn. "Winning PR Strategies." Southwest Missouri State University, Springfield. 5 Jan. 2002.

23. TWO OR MORE LECTURES BY THE SAME SPEAKER

Alexander, John. "Origins of Classical Theory." Southwest Missouri State University, Springfield. 15 Jan. 2000.

—. "Systems Theory." Southwest Missouri State University, Springfield. 10 Feb. 2000.

—. "Weick's Model of Organizing." Southwest Missouri State University, Springfield. 15 Feb. 2000.

24. FILM

The basic format for a film includes: title of film; director; distributor; and year. You may include other data that is pertinent.

The Four Seasons. Dir. Alan Alda. With Alan Alda, Carol Burnett, Len Carious, Sandy Dennis, Rita Moreno, Jack Weston, and Bess Armstrong. Universal, 1981.

The Breakfast Club. Dir. John Hughes. With Emilio Estevez, Judd Nelson, Molly Ringwald, Anthony Hall, and Ally Sheedy. Universal, 1985.

25. TELEVISION PROGRAM

The basic format for a television program includes: program title; network; local station on which you saw the program; the city; and date of broadcast. Include the episode or segment title if readily available.

CBS Evening News. CBS. KOLR, Springfield. 25 Oct. 2002.

CNN Headline News. CNN. CNN, Springfield. 16 Jan. 2002.

26. RADIO BROADCAST

The basic format for a radio broadcast includes: program title; network; local station on which you heard the program; the city; and date of broadcast.

All Things Considered. NPR. KSMU, Springfield. 24 Oct. 2002.

Morning Edition. NPR. KSMU, Springfield. 2 Jan. 2002.

27. ENCYCLOPEDIA OR DICTIONARY

The basic format for citing an article in an encyclopedia includes: article title; title of encyclopedia; edition; and year.

"Television." Encyclopedia Britannica. 15th ed. 1997.

28. WORLD WIDE WEB (WWW)

WWW pages usually provide all information necessary for correct MLA citation. In some cases, authors for a particular web page are not identified. The webmaster or system administrator of the web site may be viewed as the editor for that particular site. The following examples illustrate how various web pages should be cited.

Snyder, Alfred, Ed. "The Academy." Debate Central. University of Vermont.

    5 May 1998 <http://debate.uvm.edu/academy.html>.

Young, Jeffrey. "Of Washington Tries a Soft Sell to Woo Profesors to

    Technology." The Chronicle of Higher Education. 28 May 1999. 1 June 1999

    <http://www.chronicle.com/weekly/v45/i38/38a02301.htm>

29. ELECTRONIC COLLECTION

"AECT Publications." Association for Educational Communications and

Technology Home Page. 27 April 1998. Association for Educational

Communications and Technology. 5 May 1998

<http://204.252.76.75:80/Pubs/aectpubs.html>.

Oetting, Dan. "Eugene Debs: The Issue." Douglass: Archives of American

Public Address. 14 April 1998. Northwestern University. 5 May 1998

<http://douglass.speech.nwu.edu/debs_a80.htm>.

Trent, Judith. "An Invitation to Play a Role In NCA's Governance." National

Communication Association Home Page. 1998. National Communication

Association. 5 May

1998<http://www.natcom.org/aboutNCA/leadership/Invitation.html>.

30. DISCUSSION LIST

Driver, Dutch. "Applying Communication to COMGRADS." Online posting.

12 May 1998. COMGRADS Hotline <COMGRADS@CIOS.org>.

Moreale, Sherry. "NCA Poster Session Task Force Report." Online posting.

11 May 1998. CRTNET News <crtnet@natcom.org>.

31. ELECTRONIC MAIL (E-MAIL)

Olson, Loreen. "Worthwhile Competition." E-mail to the author. 27 April
2002.
Titsworth, Scott. "Response to John Bourhis." E-mail to the author. 8 Jan. 2002.

32. ARTICLE IN AN ONLINE PUBLICATION

The basic format for citing an online article includes all of the information for
citing a printed article plus the date of access and the URL.

Labaton, Stephen. "Media Companies Succeed in Easing Ownership Limits."

New York Times on the Web. 16 April 2001. 1 May 2001

<http://www.nytimes.com/2001/04/16/business/16MEDI.html>.

33. ONLINE BOOK

The basic format for an online book includes all of the information required for a printed book plus the date of access and the URL.

Kelly, Kevin. <u>Out of Control</u>. 1994. 2 May 2002 <http://www.well.com/user/kk/

OutOfControl/>.

PREPARING THE LIST OF WORKS CITED

The list of works cited appears at the end of the paper. Begin the list on a new page and number each page. Continue with the page numbers of the text. The title "Works Cited" appears centered at the top of the page. Double-space between the title and the first entry. Begin each entry flush with the left margin. If the entry runs more than one line in length, indent the second and each subsequent line of the entry five spaces from the left margin. Double-space the entire list, both between and within entries.

Arrange the entries in the list of works cited in alphabetical order by the author's last name. If the author's name is unknown, alphabetize the entry by the first word of the title other than "A," "An," and "The." For example: "The Recession is Coming" would be alphabetized under "R" in the list of works cited.

In citing two or more works by the same author in the works cited list, cite the author's name in the first entry only. Thereafter, use three hyphens (—) followed by a period, skip two spaces, and give the title.

MLA RULE BOX 10

Jones 8

Works Cited

McNeil, Stacy. "Classical Theory." Southwest Missouri State University, Springfield. 15 Sept. 2002.

---. "Systems Theory." Southwest Missouri State University, Springfield. 23 Oct. 2002.

Wilmot, William and Joyce Hocker. <u>Interpersonal Conflict</u>. 6th ed. New York: McGraw-Hill.

CHAPTER FIVE
A CONDENSED APA STYLE GUIDE

FORMATTING THE TEXT OF YOUR PAPER

TYPING

Unless otherwise instructed, all written work submitted for evaluation must be typed. The type must be clear, dark, and easily readable. Laser quality output has become the minimum acceptable standard for instructors as well as prospective employers. Use only standard typefaces such as Courier or Prestige Elite (standard typewriter faces), Helvetica or Times Roman (standard word-processing type faces) or their equivalents and standard type sizes (ten or twelve point). Only type on one side of the paper. Never use "fancy" or unusual fonts. Do not justify the right margin.

PAPER

Use only heavy white, 8.5 by 11 inch bond paper. Never submit any work typed on erasable or "onion skin" paper. If you use erasable paper, have a high-quality photocopy made on heavy white, 8.5 by 11 inch bond paper and submit the photocopy to your instructor. Keep the original copy for your files.

INDEX TO APA RULE BOXES

APA RULE BOX 1	Use "p" and "pp." to indicate page references, 58
APA RULE BOX 2	Using the ampersand "&" instead of "and," 59
APA RULE BOX 3	Use of primary and secondary sources, 62
APA RULE BOX 4	Capitalizing in the title of a book, 64
APA RULE BOX 5	Capitalizing in article and journal titles, 65
APA RULE BOX 6	Use quotation marks and underlining in titles, 66
APA RULE BOX 7	When to document a source, 68

MARGINS

The newest edition of APA allows you to set your margins at either 1 inch or 1.5 inches top, bottom, left and right. Consult your instructor to see if she has a particular preference. Whichever size margins you choose, be consistent throughout the entire manuscript. Nothing should appear within the margins. Indent the first word of each paragraph five to seven spaces from the left margin. Quotations in excess of 40 words should be indented five spaces from the left margin, double-spaced, and without the usual paragraph indentation. Quotations in excess of 40 words and more than one paragraph in length should have the second and each additional paragraph indented five spaces from the new margin.

LINE SPACING

Your paper should be double-spaced throughout, including the heading, title, text, quotations, and references page.

Magic Kingdom   1

Running head: MAGIC KINGDOM

Entering and Exiting the Magic Kingdom:

How Metaphors Are Used During the Organizational Assimilation

Process at Disney World

John Doe

Concordia College

TITLE PAGE

APA requires that your paper have a title page. The components of a title page are: the title of your paper, your name, institutional affiliation, and a running head. The title must also appear centered at the top of the first page of your paper followed by two spaces before the text of the paper begins. In APA, the preferred form of an author's name is first name, middle initial, and last name. Institutional affiliation refers to where the author(s) conducted the research. This includes your school. The running head is an abbreviated title that is printed at the top of the pages of a published manuscript to identify the article for readers. On your title page, type the running head in uppercase letters, flush left two lines below the pagination line. Beginning with the title, type the remaining information centered on the page, as shown in the example title page and in the sample papers in the appendixes.

PAGINATION

All scholarly writing requires pagination. Number all of the pages consecutively throughout the manuscript. Page "1" of the manuscript is the title page. Place all pagination in the upper right-hand corner, 1-12 inches from the top and 1-12 inches from the right of the page — depending on which margin size you have chosen. Remember, keep the margin area clear so your instructor has a place to make comments. To identify the manuscript, type the first two or three words from the title in the upper right-hand corner five spaces to the left of the page number. Do not punctuate the page number in any way.

	Magic Kingdom 1

BINDING

Unless otherwise instructed, neatly staple the pages of your paper together in the upper left hand corner. Do not tape, pin, or tear the corner(s) to bind the pages of your paper together. Unless specifically instructed to do so, do not submit your paper in a binder of any kind. Such bindings often make it difficult for instructors to easily grade your paper.

ABSTRACTS

APA requires an abstract for all papers/articles being submitted to a convention for presentation or journal for review and possible publication. Normally, this requirement is waived for the typical undergraduate paper. However, in special cases, your instructor may require that you write an abstract for your paper.

An abstract provides a comprehensive but brief (75-100 word) summary of the contents of a paper/article. The abstract should be descriptive of the contents of the work cited not evaluative. Do not indent the first word of the abstract.

An abstract for a theoretical article should contain the following information:

1. a concise statement of the topic;
2. a description of the purpose, thesis, or central construct that guides the work;
3. the sources of information used in the book or article; and
4. the conclusions and implications of the book or article as suggested by the author(s).

An abstract for an empirical study should contain the following information:

1. the research question(s) or hypothesis(es) studied;
2. a description of the subjects employed in the study including: number, type, age, sex, and selection procedures;
3. a description of the experimental method(s) employed;
4. the results of the study including significance levels where appropriate; and
5. the conclusions and implications of the research as suggested by the author(s).

Abstract

A meta-analysis of 183 experiments comparing the effect sizes of measurement techniques for assessing the effectiveness of public speaking anxiety treatments was conducted. The comparison showed differences between self-report, observer, and physiological measurement techniques. However, no interaction was observed between the type of therapy and the type of measurement technique. The implications for measuring public speaking anxiety and the classroom application of the results are considered.

CITING SOURCES IN THE TEXT OF YOUR PAPER

APA style uses parenthetical references for citing sources. Parenthetical references are placed within the text of the paper rather than at the bottom of each page (footnotes) or at the end of the paper (endnotes). The basic format for an APA parenthetical reference is: (author's last name, followed by a space, and the year in which the work was published).

For example:

> Surprisingly, television probably is more conservative than other
>
> media in its portrayal of family life (Albada, 2000).

As a way of adding variety to your citations, mention the author's name in the text and include the year parenthetically. For example:

> Albada (2000) suggests that television probably is more
>
> conservative than other media in its portrayal of family life.

When citing an entire work, the most elegant citation is to include the author (and possibly the work) in the text and include the year parenthetically.

> In The Corporate Culture Survival Guide, Edgar Schein (1999)
>
> provides a layperson's guide to understanding organizational
>
> culture.

or

> Schein (1999) provides a layperson's guide to understanding
>
> organizational culture.

When citing an English translation of a non-English work, include the author's name, the original date of publication, and the date of the English translation. For example:

> The French were not the first to make this observation (Foucault,
>
> 1969/1982).

When a reference contains a direct quotation, APA requires that a page number(s) be included in the parenthetical reference. The basic format for an APA parenthetical reference for a direct quotation is: (author's last name, space, date, space, "p." space, followed by the page number(s). For example:

"The easiest level to observe when you go into an organization is

that of artifacts: what you see, hear, and feel as you hang around"

(Schein, 1999, p. 15).

APA RULE BOX 1

APA makes use of "p." to indicate a single page reference or "pp." to indicate that a quotation appears on more than one page of the cited material. Also note that the concluding punctuation appears at the end of an extended quotation BEFORE the parenthetical reference. In APA, no punctuation follows the parenthetical reference for an extended quotation.

The same rules apply when citing a direct quotation from a source with two authors. If the work cited has two authors, include the names of both authors each time the reference occurs in the text.

"Perhaps the most essential feature of human interaction is that it

involves adaptation" (White & Burgoon, 2001, p. 9).

If the work cited has three or more authors, include the names of all authors the first time a reference is made to the work. In subsequent references, include only the first author's name followed by "et al." (meaning "and others"), followed by a space and the date.
First reference:

"The assumption is that persons dishonest during the employment

interview will be dishonest on the job" (Mattson, Allen, Ryan, &

Miller, 2000, p. 148).

Each subsequent reference:

"Although further research is warranted, this study provides

the foundation on which to build a more complete understanding

of deception as both an interpersonal and an organizational

phenomenon" (Mattson et al., 2000, p. 155).

APA RULE BOX 2

Notice that in the parenthetical reference the ampersand or "&" sign is used. In parenthetical references and in the list of references, APA uses the ampersand instead of spelling out "and." In the text of the paper, always use "and."

When a direct quotation exceeds forty words in length, <u>APA</u> requires that the quotation be "set-off" from the rest of the text. Introduce and cite the quotation as you would normally, omit the quotation marks, indent the entire quotation five spaces from the left margin, and write it in block form within the text. If the quotation exceeds forty words in length and contains more than one paragraph, indent the first word of each subsequent paragraph five spaces from the new left margin. For example:

> The social sciences are another matter.
>
> While theories about human behavior often cast their predictions in cause-and-effect terms, a certain humility on the part of the theorist is advisable. Even the best theory may only be able to talk in terms of probability and tendencies – not absolute certainty. (Griffin, 2000, p. 23)

Note that the punctuation appears at the end of the block quotation, not at the end of the citation for the quotation. Do not include any punctuation at the end of the citation for a block quotation.

When citing a single work by an author of two or more works in the text of your paper, include the suffixes a, b, c, and so forth after the year.

> In addition to critiquing data collection methods (Shrum, 1999a), the author has examined the cultivation effect (Shrum, 1999b) and the interaction of television programs and advertisements (Shrum, 1999c).

CITING SOURCES OBTAINED ELECTRONICALLY

Increasingly, students and faculty are making use of electronic sources of information when conducting research. The days of card catalogs and wandering aimlessly through dusty library shelves looking for sources of information are over. Even the phrase "card catalog" may be meaningless for many contemporary writers. Current editions of the Modern Language Association and the American Psychological Association manuals do not include conventions for citing information obtained via the four most commonly used sources of electronic information: WWW pages, electronic collections, discussion lists, and electronic mail. The most recent edition of the APA Manual uses Li and Crane's format for citing electronic citations. A summary of their suggestions may be found on-line at the following address:

http://www.apa.org/journals/webref.html

The goal of any form of citation is to allow the information you have used in your manuscript to be retrieved again; either by you or someone else interested in your topic. Your citation must be complete and must allow someone else to retrace your steps in obtaining the information electronically. With electronic citations, it is especially important that punctuation and capitalization be accurate in the address. Use standard APA rules and conventions for citing authors and sources discussed previously in this section, including rules for capitalization. Although there are no accepted APA conventions for citing electronic works, here are some suggestions based on Li and Crane's work:

1. Identify the name of the author, editor, compiler, or translator of the source (if available), reversed for alphabetizing and followed by an abbreviation (i.e., Ed.) if appropriate.
2. Provide the date of publication or of the last update if available. For discussion group postings or electronic mail, indicate the date of the message. This date should be enclosed in parentheses. If no date is available, indicate "No date" in parentheses.
3. Identify the title of the work whether it be a speech, web page, or article. If it is a posting from a discussion list or electronic mail, provide the title from the subject line.
4. Provide the name of the web site, discussion group, or other electronic source you are referencing. This title should be underlined.
5. Brackets containing a description of the electronic medium (e.g., Online, CD-ROM, etc.) should follow the title of the web site, discussion list, or CD ROM you are referencing.
6. Name the institution, sponsoring organization, or discussion group responsible for producing the source.

7. Provide a complete electronic address, URL, or other information about availability including any commands necessary for retrieval from a server.
8. In brackets, indicate the date that the material was accessed by the researcher.

In general, these guidelines require electronic sources to follow the following format that can be readily adapted to various forms of electronic material:

Author's last name, first initial. (Date of publication, revision, or indicate no date) Title of specific article. In Name of Web Site or Electronic Source [medium]. Name of Sponsoring Institution. Available: complete electronic address and other information about availability [access date].

When using this format to cite electronic sources like web pages or electronic mail messages, minor adaptations are necessary. What follows are examples of commonly cited sources in proper APA format.

PRIMARY VERSUS SECONDARY SOURCE MATERIAL

To properly evaluate sources, you need to determine whether or not your supporting material is from a primary or secondary source. Primary source material (direct) refers to research, information or opinion as it was originally presented or published. Secondary source material (indirect) is a summary of research, information or opinion prepared by someone other than the original creator. If someone conducts a study that examines the relationship between communication apprehension and academic achievement and publishes the results of the study, that publication is a primary source. If a graduate student locates a copy of the printed article on communication apprehension and academic achievement and uses information from the article in a course paper, the graduate student's paper is a secondary source. When you cite a textbook, you are often relying on a secondary source, the author of the textbook who is summarizing work done by others. You are trusting that the author of the text has read and analyzed primary source material and is accurately and objectively summarizing that material in the text.

APA RULE BOX 3

As a general rule it is always preferable to rely on primary versus secondary source material in your writing. Reliance on primary source material results in scholarship that is more credible and persuasive. For this reason, graduate students may be required to use only primary source material in their scholarly writing, particularly for the thesis and dissertation.

CITING A SECONDARY SOURCE IN YOUR MANUSCRIPT

To document to the reader that you are relying upon secondary source material in your manuscript, identify the primary (direct) source and use "as cited in" preceding the secondary (indirect) source in which you found the material. In the list of references, only include the source you consulted (secondary source), not the primary source you are citing.

Celia Green once wrote that, "The way to do research is to attack the facts

at the point of greatest astonishment" (as cited in Reinhard, 2001, p. 183).

In this example Celia Green is the primary source and John Reinhard is the secondary source. In the list of references the citation would read:

Scholarly Writing 12

References

Reinhard, J. (2001). Introduction to communication research (3rd ed.). Boston: McGraw-Hill.

SAMPLE APA ENTRIES

BOOKS

1. BOOK WITH ONE AUTHOR

Reinard, J. C. (2001). Introduction to communication research (3rd ed.). New York: McGraw-Hill.

Tubbs, S. L. (2001). A systems approach to small group interaction (7th ed.). New York: McGraw-Hill.

2. BOOK WITH TWO AUTHORS

Ivy, D. K., & Backlunck, P. (2000). <u>Exploring genderspeak: Personal effectiveness in gender communication</u> (2nd ed.). New York: McGraw-Hill.

Wilmot, W. W., & Hocker, J. L. (2001). <u>Interpersonal conflict</u> (6th ed.). New York: McGraw-Hill.

APA RULE BOX 4

How do I know which words to capitalize in the title of a book?

In book titles and subtitles, capitalize the first word of the title and of the subtitle, if any. All other words begin with a lowercase letter. Separate titles from subtitles with a colon. Include any other punctuation that is part of the title. Underline the entire title, including the ending punctuation. For example:

<u>Effective group discussion: Theory and practice.</u>

---

3. BOOK WITH THREE AUTHORS

Brilhart, J. K., Galanes, G. J., & Adams, K. (2001). <u>Effective group discussion: Theory and practice</u> (10th ed.). New York: McGraw-Hill.

Bourhis, J., & Adams, C., Titsworth, S., & Harter, L. (2001). <u>A style manual for communication majors</u> (1st ed.). New York: McGraw-Hill.

4. TWO OR MORE BOOKS BY THE SAME AUTHOR

Tubbs, S. L. (1993). <u>Self-directed teams.</u> Ann Arbor, MI: U-Train.

Tubbs, S. L. (2001). <u>A systems approach to small group interaction</u> (7thed.). New York: McGraw-Hill.

5. BOOK WITH AN EDITOR

Kreps, G. L. (Ed.). (1993). <u>Sexual harassment: Communication implications.</u> Creskill, NJ: Hampton.

6. BOOK WITH TWO EDITORS

Jablin, F. M., & Putnam, L. L. (Eds.). (2001). <u>The new handbook of organizational communication: Advances in theory, research, and methods.</u> Thousand Oaks, CA: Sage.

7. AN EDITION OTHER THAN THE FIRST

Griffin, E. (2000). <u>A first look at communication theory</u> (4th ed.). New York: McGraw-Hill.

8. A WORK IN A BOOK

Eisenberg, E. M., & Riley, P. (2001). Organizational culture. In F. M. Jablin & L. L. Putnam (Eds.), <u>The new handbook of organizational communication: Advances in theory, research, and methods</u> (pp. 291-322). Thousand Oaks, CA: Sage.

APA RULE BOX 5

How do I know which words to capitalize in article and journal titles?

Capitalize the first word of an article title and subtitle, if any. Separate a title from its subtitle with a colon. For example:

Interpersonal deception: Communication apprehension as a contributing factor.

Give the journal title in full. Capitalize all nouns, pronouns, adjectives and adverbs. Do not capitalize coordinating conjunctions (and, but, for, nor, or) or prepositions introducing phrases (of, before, in, to). Do not capitalize an article (a, an, the) unless it is the first word of a journal title. Underline the title including the ending punctuation. For example:

<u>Quarterly Journal of Speech.</u>

---

9. A TRANSLATION

Aristotle. (1954). The Rhetoric (W. R. Roberts, Trans.). New York: Modern Library. (Original work published 330 B.C.E.)

Foucault, M. (1982). The archaeology of knowledge (A. M. S. Smith, Trans.). New York: Pantheon Books. (Original work published 1969).

ARTICLES

The basic format for an article entry includes: author's name; date of publication; title of article; name of periodical; volume number; and page numbers.

10. ARTICLE WITH ONE AUTHOR

Harwood, J. (2000). Communication media use in the grandparent-grandchild relationship. Journal of Communication, 50, 56-78.

Barge, J. K. (2001). Practical theory as mapping, engaged reflection, and transformative practice. Communication Theory, 11, 5-13.

11. ARTICLE WITH TWO AUTHORS

Floyd, K., & Morman, M. T. (2000). Affection received from fathers as a predictor of men's affection with their own sons: Tests of the modeling and compensation hypotheses. Communication Monographs, 67, 347-367.

Tewksbury, D., & Althaus, S. L. (2000). An examination of motivations for using the World Wide Web. Communication Research Reports, 17, 127-138.

APA RULE BOX 6

When citing an article in a periodical, when do I use quotation marks and when do I underline?

Quotation marks are never used in APA unless they are part of the punctuation of a title. Do not underline article titles. Underline book, journal and film titles followed by a period. Underline the period following the title. Underline the commas before and after volume numbers in a periodical citation.

---

12. ARTICLE WITH THREE OR MORE AUTHORS

Guerrero, L. K., Jones, S. M., & Burgoon, J. K. (2000). Responses to nonverbal intimacy change in romantic dyads: Effects of behavioral valence and degree of behavioral change on nonverbal and verbal reactions. Communication Monographs, 67, 325-346.

Boster, F. J., Cameron, K. A., Campo, S., Lia, W., Lillie, J. K., Baker, E. M., & Yun, K. A. (2000). The persuasive effects of statistical evidence in the presence of exemplars. Communication Studies, 3, 296-306.

13. ARTICLE IN A MONTHLY OR BIMONTHLY PERIODICAL

Holland, R. J., & Potter, L. R. (2000, August). Customer vs. audience: When worlds collide. Communication World, 17, 15.

Make the right impact with technology. (2000, October). Training, 37, 1.

14. ARTICLE IN A WEEKLY OR BIWEEKLY PERIODICAL

Berman, D. (1998, November 2). Calling all raconteurs: Executive Communications Group holds executive storytelling seminars as a communication tool. Business Week, 6.

Slatalla, M. (2000, September 11). Brotherly love: A study suggests ways to rear siblings who will get along now – and for the rest of their lives. Time, 156, 122.

NEWSPAPERS

The basic format for a newspaper entry includes: author's name; date; article title; name of newspaper; and page.

15. SIGNED ARTICLE FROM A DAILY NEWSPAPER

Hundley, T. (2001, April 1). Milosevic arrested after 26-hour crisis. Chicago Tribune, p. 1A.

Flemming, P. (2001, April 1). Problems linger from AWG strike. Springfield News-Leader, p. 1A.

16. UNSIGNED ARTICLE FROM A DAILY NEWSPAPER

Bomb kills 11 at concert in Sri Lanka. (2001, April 1). Chicago Tribune, p. A8.

17. SIGNED EDITORIAL FROM A DAILY NEWSPAPER

Reilly, W. K. (2001, April 1). New York Times, p. A30.

Veneman, A. M. (2001, March 31). USA Today, p. 18A.

18. UNSIGNED EDITORIAL FROM A DAILY NEWSPAPER

A vision for city's future. (2001, April 1). Springfield News-Leader, p. 10A.

MANUSCRIPTS

19. UNPUBLISHED MANUSCRIPT

Adams, C. (2001). Instructors' use of e-mail and student perceptions of immediacy. Unpublished manuscript.

20. UNPUBLISHED PAPER PRESENTED AT A MEETING

Harter, L. M. (2000, November). Images of sexual harassment in popular culture: Prime time portrayals of organizational diversity. Paper presented at the annual meeting of the National Communication Association, Seattle, WA.

21. PERSONAL COMMUNICATION

Personal communications may include sources such as letters, memos, e-mail, messages from electronic bulletin boards, telephone conversations, interviews, and class lectures. Because they are not retrievable sources, APA does not include personal communications in the reference list. Instead, cite personal communications in the text only. Your instructor may give you specific instructions about citing certain non-retrievable sources such as interviews or class lectures. Absent any specific instructions, personal communications should be cited in the text as in these examples. Give the initials and surname of the communicator, and provide as exact a date as possible.

> (J. B. Bourhis, personal communication, April 8, 2001)

> (C. H. Adams, personal communication, January 28, 2001)

22. LECTURE

See the format for Personal Communication above.

23. FILM

The basic format for a film includes: director's name; date; film title; [Film]; place of production; and studio.

> Schamus, J. (Producer), Hope, T. (Producer), & Lee, A. (Director). (1997).

The ice storm [Film]. Los Angeles: Fox Searchlight Productions.

24. TELEVISION PROGRAM

The basic format for a television program includes: program title; date of broadcast; and network. If the television program was produced locally, include place of origin and station. Include the episode or segment title if readily available.

> CBS evening news. (2001, May 23). CBS.

> CNN headline news. (2001, April 21). CNN.

25. RADIO BROADCAST

The basic format for a radio broadcast includes: program title; date of broadcast; and network. If the radio broadcast was produced locally, replace network with place of origin and station.

> All things considered. (2001, May 23). National Public Radio.

> Morning edition. (2001, April 21). National Public Radio.

26. ENCYCLOPEDIA OR DICTIONARY

> Bergman, P. G. (1993). Relativity. In The new encyclopedia Britannica

(Vol. 26, pp. 501-508). Chicago: Encyclopedia Britannica.

27. WORLD WIDE WEB (WWW)

WWW pages usually provide all information necessary for correct APA citation. In some cases, authors for a particular web page are not identified. The webmaster or system administrator of the web site may be viewed as the Aeditor@ for that particular site. The following examples illustrate how various web pages should be cited.

Gaudino, J. (Ed.). (No date). About NCA [On-line]. National

Communication Association. Available: http://www.natcom.org/AboutNCA/

about_nca1.htm [2001, April 1].

Heflin, B. (2000, February/March). Christianity deconstructed #4:

Deconstructing deconstruction. In Stranger Things Magazine [On-line].

Available: http://www.strangerthingsmag.com/decon4.html [2001, April 1].

28. ELECTRONIC COLLECTION

National Archives and Records Administration. (2001, January 11).

Memorandum of understanding between the National Archives and Records

Administration and the Executive Office of the President. In National Archives

and Records Administration Home Page [On-line]. National Archives and

Records Administration. Available: http://www.nara.gov/nara/president/

ARMSOU.html [2001, April 1].

Milward, S. (Ed.). (2001). Computer-mediated Communication. In ACA

Studies Center [On-line]. American Communication Association. Available:

http://www.uark.edu/~aca/studies/cmc.html [2001, April 1].

29. DISCUSSION LIST

When citing discussion lists the availability information should include any necessary commands required to retrieve the message from the discussion listserv. For example, the listserv at the University of Pittsburgh allows access to archives of the CRTNET discussion group by using the "index" command. If such a command is not provided, the "help" command may be used to get information on how to access archives. The following examples illustrate how these commands may be included in citations.

Driver, D. (1988, May 12). Applying communication to COMGRADS. COMGRADS Hotline [On-line]. Discussion group posting. Available E-Mail: LISTSERV@CIOS.org/help [1988, May 12].

Moreale, S. (1988, May 11). NCA poster session task force report. CRTNET News [On-line]. Available E-Mail: LISTSERV@lists.psu.edu/index [1998, May 11].

30. ELECTRONIC MAIL (E-MAIL)

Olson, L. (olson@server.edu). (1998, April 27). Worthwhile essay competition (fwd). E-mail to Scott Titsworth (scott@server.edu).

Levine, T. (tl@server.edu). (1998, February 5). 1-tailed F=s. E-mail to Scott Titsworth (scott@server.edu).

31. ARTICLE IN AN ONLINE PUBLICATION

The basic format for citing an online article includes all of the information for citing a printed article plus the date of access and the URL.

Labaton, S. (2001, April 16). Media companies succeed in easing ownership limits." New York Times on the Web. Retrieved May 1, 2001 from the World Wide Web: http://www.nytimes.com/2001/04/16/business/16MEDI.html

32. ONLINE BOOK

The basic format for an online book includes all of the information required for a printed book plus the date of access and the URL.

Kelly, K. (1994). Out of control. New York: Addison Wesley. Retrieved May 2, 2002 from the World Wide Web: http://www.well.com/user/kk/OutOfControl/

PREPARING THE LIST OF REFERENCES

The list of references appears at the end of the paper. Begin the list on a new page and number each page. Continue with the page numbers of the text. The title "References" appears centered at the top of the page. The title "Reference" is used if there is only one reference in the paper. Double-space between the title and the first entry. Begin each entry indented five spaces from the left margin. If the entry runs more than one line in length, the second and each subsequent line should be flush left. Double-space the entire list, both between and within entries.

Arrange the entries in the list of references in alphabetical order by the author's last name. If the author's name is unknown, alphabetize the entry by the first word of the title other than "A," "An," and "The." "The Recession is Coming" would be alphabetized under "R" in the list of references. When ordering several entries by the same author, arrange the entries chronologically from earliest to latest. When ordering entries with the same first author and different second authors, arrange the entries alphabetically by second author. Single author entries precede multiple-author entries beginning with the same surname. When listing multiple works by the same author with the same date of publication, arrange your entries on the reference page alphabetically by title ignoring "a, and, the" when they appear as the first word in a title.

Television Viewing 8

References

Shrum, L. J. (1999a). The effect of data-collection method on the cultivation effect: Implications for the heuristic processing model of cultivation effects. Paper presented at the meeting of the International Communication Association, San Francisco, CA.

Shrum, L. J. (1999b). The relationship of television viewing with attitude strength and extremity: Implications for the cultivation effect. Media Psychology, 1, 3-25.

Shrum, L. J. (1999c). Television and persuasion: Effects of the programs between the ads. Psychology and Marketing, 16, 119-140.

My Paper 8

References

Craig, R. T. (1995).

Craig, R. T., & Tracy, K. (1995).

APPENDIX A
Model Paper Following <u>MLA</u> Guidelines

"Diversity" in the Rhetoric and
Practices of Planned Parenthood

Rachel M. Deibert

Communication 301
Dr. Lynn Harter
26 March 2001

Pagination appears on every page of the manuscript, including the title page as page 1. Pagination includes your last name, two spaces and the page number ½ inch from the top and right margin.

Center your title at the top of the page using upper and lower case letters.

If your instructor requires a separate, formal title page, use this as a model.

Include the title of the course, your instructor's name and the date the manuscript is due. Note the format for date in MLA is Day Month Year.

"Diversity" in the Rhetoric and

Practices of Planned Parenthood

In organizational settings, "diversity" is a term often used in reference to people of different races, sexes, economic standings, sexual orientations, levels of physical and mental abilities, ages, and religions. Communication scholars often embrace a social constructionist perspective that recognizes notions of diversity as created and maintained through discursive interactions (e.g., Allen 143). In other words, our societal understandings of "diversity" emerge from how we talk about and enact, through a variety of practices, diversity. In this essay, I explore the rhetoric and practices of Planned Parenthood, an institution that has attempted to create an organizational culture that accepts and appreciates diversity. While Planned Parenthood seeks to provide reproductive care to a "diverse" clientele, upon closer examination the organization's practices fall short of their rhetorical vision and potentially disempower diverse populations.

Margaret Sanger established Planned Parenthood in 1916. Sanger was a leading activist in the early 1900's for women's reproductive rights. She maintained that women should have full control over their reproductive health, that every child should be wanted, and that sex should be pleasurable for both men and women. Despite jail time and public scrutiny, the web page for Planned Parenthood explains that Sanger was a driving force in the legalization of birth control and other forms of contraceptives. Planned Parenthood has evolved into an organization whose "mission" is to provide a number of reproductive-related health services including pregnancy counseling, screening for sexually transmitted diseases, and contraceptive prescriptions, while creating an environment that values and respects "diversity."

If your instructor requires a separate title page, repeat the title of the paper centered at the top of the first page using upper and lower case letters.

Indent the first word of each paragraph of the manuscript 1/2 inch or approximately five spaces.

"e.g." is an abbreviation for the Latin phrase, *exempli gratia* (for example).

Do not justify the text, use a ragged right-hand margin.

Observe one inch margins top, bottom, left and right.

Deibert 3

Mission statements are one way that leaders attempt to cultivate both an "identity" and "image" for organizations (Fairhurst, Monroe and Neuwirth 245). Mission statements articulate core values and principles that presumably guide members' choices and behaviors. Mission statements are "the corporate version of an ego ideal, a standard by which the corporation is supposed to measure itself" (Fairhurst, Monroe and Neuwirth 246). Mission statements are an increasingly popular form of corporate communication and are often expressed to both internal and external audiences. By expressing a formal ideology or belief system of the organization, mission statements ideally function to create "identification" between members, clients, and the organization (Cheney 360).

In its mission statement, Planned Parenthood creates an image of an organization that embraces diversity. "Planned Parenthood believes in the fundamental right of each individual, throughout the world, to manage his or her fertility. We believe that respect and value for diversity in all aspects of our organization are essential to our well being" (Planned Parenthood "Home Page"). While Planned Parenthood's mission statement is strategically ambiguous (Eisenberg 229), it does set a standard from which to judge its practices – a standard valuing "diversity." If we are to assume that Planned Parenthood's mission statement is a vision for organizational decision-making and practices of the organization, we would expect to find practices and discourse that targets diverse individuals and their reproductive needs.

Planned Parenthood's mission is very vague in terms of how the organization "respects" and "values" diversity. In fact, it is unclear if and how care is provided to diverse

> When using a direct quotation, word-for-word, put the cited material in quotation marks. Put the last quotation mark at the end of the quoted material.

> Work with three authors; in MLA use "and." Note no punctuation between authors and page reference.

> Single author in-text citation.

> In-text citation of material obtained from the internet. Reader can find the complete citation by referring to the list of Works Cited.

individuals (e.g., men and women). Current programs, advertisements and literature provided by Planned Parenthood better illustrate the amount of care diverse individuals are granted. While the programs of Planned Parenthood do feature elements consistent with their mission statement, care is largely provided to women. Pregnancy counseling is provided to women in the comfort of a doctor's office. Counseling for fathers of unwanted pregnancies or even wanted pregnancies is not provided. Planned Parenthood also serves as a leader of women's rights legislation and has supported bills and laws that exclude men from pregnancy decisions.

Trace evidence available in popular culture also illustrates how Planned Parenthood targets primarily women in marketing their services. One of the most current advertisements of Planned Parenthood focuses on the distribution of Emergency Contraception. Emergency Contraception, also known as The Morning After Pill, has become one of the most controversial drugs of the decade. Planned Parenthood has provided aid for women to obtain the drug. The advertisement features models and actress Stacy Dash (Clueless) scantily clad with the phrase, "Accidents happen … If you have unprotected sex. You have 72 hours to reduce your risk of getting pregnant" (Planned Parenthood "Home Page"). Other literature that Planned Parenthood distributes clearly targets females. Throughout their literature they use hypothetical examples that ignore the male voice in reproductive-related scenarios. Rather, the discourse emphasizes the internal monologue of women in hypothetical situations.

Planned Parenthood was established at a time when women received little rights and choices in carrying children and other reproductive manners. The organization was successful in its original mission to empower women. However, the formal

rhetoric (i.e., the mission statement) of the organization
has evolved. The mission statement suggests that the
organization's "well-being" is dependent upon valuing and
respecting diversity. Yet, the practices and other discourse
of the organization appear to contradict this mission.
In fact, through its discourse Planned Parenthood potentially
undermines the importance of men in their organization and
their role in reproductive decision-making.

"i.e." is an abbreviation for the Latin phrase, *id est* (that is).

Collectively, the discourse of Planned Parenthood
perpetuates the image that men are not to be held responsible
for reproductive decisions. This reflects and perpetuates
contemporary ideologies that place the responsibility of
protected sex, adoption, abortion and other such decisions
exclusively on the shoulders of women. This ideology
potentially creates an organizational environment that does
not, in fact, value diversity in the form of welcoming men.
In this sense, Planned Parenthood falls short of its current
mission.

What is even more dangerous is the lack of information
on men's health issues. Planned Parenthood does provide
screening for sexually transmitted diseases for both sexes
and distributes condoms. However, Planned Parenthood
does little else to value and respect the reproductive needs
and responsibilities of men. Nor does the discourse of
Planned Parenthood recognize men as active agents in
reproductive decision-making. It should come as no surprise
that few men regard Planned Parenthood to be a source of
information on their reproductive health. The clientele of
Planned Parenthood is typically comprised of women
without health insurance or those interested in the privacy
that the organization provides (Planned Parenthood "Home
Page"). Without yearly examinations, men are at a greater

risk of developing irreversible health problems. If men do not receive proper screening, they can easily spread sexually transmitted diseases to their partners and the unborn. If men are not included in counseling sessions about reproductive decisions, they may be less likely to be committed to such decisions.

Underscoring existing literature about organizational mission statements is the acknowledged widespread failure in their implementation (Fairhurst, Jordan, Neuwirth 244). Clearly, the case of Planned Parenthood illustrates this argument. While the organization formally recognizes that their well-being depends on valuing diversity, their practices contradict this mission. Perhaps the leaders of Planned Parenthood could argue that their goal is not to serve men; rather, their goal is to empower women. If that is the case, the organization should re-evaluate its mission statement. If the organization truly does intend to address the responsibilities and roles of diverse individuals (i.e., men and women) in reproductive health care, it should re-evaluate its discourse and practices.

Deibert 7

Works Cited

Allen, Brenda. "Diversity' and Organizational

Communication." Journal of Applied Communication 23

(1995): 143-155.

Cheney, George. "On the Various and Changing Meanings

of Organizational Membership: A Field Study of

Organizational Identification." Communication

Monographs 50 (1983): 342-362.

Eisenberg, Erik. "Ambiguity as Strategy in Organizational

Communication." Communication Monographs 51

(1984): 227-242.

Fairhurst, Gail, Jerry Jordan and Kurt Neuwirth. "Why Are

We Here? Managing the Meaning of an organizational

Mission Statement. Journal of Applied Communication

Research 25 (1997): 243-263.

Planned Parenthood. "Home Page." Planned Parenthood

Federation of America, Inc. 20 March 2001

<Http://www.plannedparenthood.org/>.

The Works Cited is a separate page of the manuscript.

"Works Cited" is centered at the top of the page using upper and lower case letters. Double space to the first entry.

Observe the same margins and pagination requirements as the rest of the manuscript.

The first line of each entry is flush with the left margin; subsequent lines are indented 1/2 inch or approximately five spaces.

APPENDIX B
Model Paper Following <u>APA</u> Guidelines

Running head: PLANNED PARENTHOOD

"Diversity" in the Rhetoric and

Practices of Planned Parenthood

Rachel M. Deibert

Minnesota State University Moorhead

In APA, pagination includes a short abbreviation of the title and the page number on every page of the manuscript, including the title page.

The running head only appears on the title page of the manuscript and is used by journal editors for publication purposes. Note the unusual use of upper and lower case letters. Students frequently make mistakes in typing the running head.

Include title, your first and last name, and your school affiliation, all double spaced using upper and lower case letters.

"Diversity" in the Rhetoric and

Practices of Planned Parenthood

In organizational settings, "diversity" is a term often used in reference to people of different races, sexes, economic standings, sexual orientations, levels of physical and mental abilities, ages, and religions. Communication scholars often embrace a social constructionist perspective that recognizes notions of diversity as created and maintained through discursive interactions (e.g., Allen, 1995). In other words, our societal understandings of "diversity" emerge from how we talk about and enact, through a variety of practices, diversity. In this essay, I explore the rhetoric and practices of Planned Parenthood, an institution that has attempted to create an organizational culture that accepts and appreciates diversity. While Planned Parenthood seeks to provide reproductive care to a "diverse" clientele, upon closer examination the organization's practices fall short of their rhetorical vision and potentially disempower diverse populations.

Margaret Sanger established Planned Parenthood in 1916. Sanger was a leading activist in the early 1900's for women's reproductive rights. She maintained that women should have full control over their reproductive health, that every child should be wanted, and that sex should be pleasurable for both men and women. Despite jail time and public scrutiny, Sanger was a driving force in the legalization of birth control and other forms of contraceptives (Planned Parenthood, 2001). Planned Parenthood has evolved into an organization whose "mission" is to provide a number of reproductive-related health services including pregnancy counseling, screening for sexually transmitted diseases, and contraceptive prescriptions, while creating an environment that values and respects "diversity."

Paginate every page of the manuscript.

Indent each new paragraph 1/2 inch or approximately five spaces. Double space all text.

In APA all text citations should include year of publication or access.

"e.g." is an abbreviation for the Latin phrase, *exempli gratia* (for example).

Do not use full justification, use a ragged right-hand margin.

In text citation for material obtained from the internet, including year of access.

Observe 1 inch margins on all sides.

Mission statements are one way that leaders attempt to cultivate both an "identity" and "image" for organizations (Fairhurst, Monroe & Neuwirth, 1997). Mission statements articulate core values and principles that presumably guide members' choices and behaviors. Fairhurst, Monroe, and Neuwirth (1997) describe mission statements as "the corporate version of an ego ideal, a standard by which the corporation is supposed to measure itself" (p. 243). Mission statements are an increasingly popular form of corporate communication and are often expressed to both internal and external audiences. By expressing a formal ideology or belief system of the organization, mission statements ideally function to create "identification" between members, clients, and the organization (Cheney, 1983).

In its mission statement, Planned Parenthood creates an image of an organization that embraces diversity. "Planned Parenthood believes in the fundamental right of each individual, throughout the world, to manage his or her fertility. We believe that respect and value for diversity in all aspects of our organization are essential to our well being" (Planned Parenthood, 2001, np). While Planned Parenthood's mission statement is strategically ambiguous (Eisenberg, 1984), it does set a standard from which to judge its practices – a standard valuing "diversity." If we are to assume that Planned Parenthood's mission statement is a vision for organizational decision-making and practices of the organization, we would expect to find practices and discourse that targets diverse individuals and their reproductive needs.

Planned Parenthood's mission is very vague in terms of how the organization "respects" and "values" diversity. In fact, it is unclear if and how care is provided to diverse individuals (e.g., men and women). Current programs,

In APA use the ampersand sign "&" instead of "and" in the in text citation.

In most cases, punctuate at the end of the citation not at the end of the material cited.

In APA use "p." for page or "pp." for inclusive pages in the citation.

Note the comma that goes after the author's name and before the year of publication.

Note the "np" meaning no page. This is a direct quotation so material must be included in quotation marks. Because the information comes from the internet, no page reference is possible and is noted using "np."

advertisements and literature provided by Planned Parenthood better illustrate the amount of care diverse individuals are granted. While the programs of Planned Parenthood do feature elements consistent with their mission statement, care is largely provided to women. Pregnancy counseling is provided to women in the comfort of a doctor's office. Counseling for fathers of unwanted pregnancies or even wanted pregnancies is not provided. Planned Parenthood also serves as a leader of women's rights legislation and has supported bills and laws that exclude men from pregnancy decisions.

Trace evidence available in popular culture also illustrates how Planned Parenthood targets primarily women in marketing its services. One of the most current advertisements of Planned Parenthood focuses on the distribution of Emergency Contraception. Emergency Contraception, also known as The Morning After Pill, has become one of the most controversial drugs of the decade. Planned Parenthood has provided aid for women to obtain the drug. The advertisement features models and actress Stacy Dash (<u>Clueless</u>) scantily clad with the phrase, "Accidents happen ... if you have unprotected sex. You have 72 hours to reduce your risk of getting pregnant" (Planned Parenthood, 2001, np). Other literature that Planned Parenthood distributes clearly targets females. Throughout their literature they use hypothetical examples that ignore the male voice in reproductive-related scenarios. Rather, the discourse emphasizes the internal monologue of women in hypothetical situations.

Planned Parenthood was established at a time when women received little rights and choices in carrying children and other reproductive manners. The organization was successful in its original mission to empower women. However, the formal rhetoric (i.e., the mission statement) of

"i.e." is an abbreviation for the Latin phrase, *id est* (that is).

the organization has evolved. The mission statement suggests that the organization's "well-being" is dependent upon valuing and respecting diversity. Yet, the practices and other discourse of the organization appear to contradict this mission. In fact, through its discourse Planned Parenthood potentially undermines the importance of men in its organization and their role in reproductive decision-making.

Collectively, the discourse of Planned Parenthood perpetuates the image that men are not to be held responsible for reproductive decisions. This reflects and perpetuates contemporary ideologies that place the responsibility of protected sex, adoption, abortion and other such decisions exclusively on the shoulders of women. This ideology potentially creates an organizational environment that does not, in fact, value diversity in the form of welcoming men. In this sense, Planned Parenthood falls short of its current mission.

What is even more dangerous is the lack of information on men's health issues. Planned Parenthood does provide screening for sexually transmitted diseases for both sexes and distributes condoms. However, Planned Parenthood does little else to value and respect the reproductive needs and responsibilities of men. Nor does the discourse of Planned Parenthood recognize men as active agents in reproductive decision-making. It should come as no surprise that few men regard Planned Parenthood to be a source of information on their reproductive health. The clientele of Planned Parenthood is typically comprised of women without health insurance or those interested in the privacy that the organization provides (Planned Parenthood, 2001). Without yearly examinations, men are at a greater risk of developing irreversible health problems. If men do not receive proper screening, they can easily spread sexually transmitted diseases to their partners and the unborn. If men are not included in counseling sessions about reproductive decisions, they may be less likely to be committed to such decisions.

Underscoring existing literature about organizational mission statements is the acknowledged widespread failure in its implementation (Fairhurst, Jordan & Neuwirth, 1997). Clearly, the case of Planned Parenthood illustrates this argument. While the organization formally recognizes that their well-being depends on valuing diversity, its practices contradict this mission. Perhaps the leaders of Planned

Parenthood could argue that their goal is not to serve men; rather, their goal is to empower women. If that is the case, the organization should re-evaluate its mission statement. If the organization truly does intend to address the responsibilities and roles of diverse individuals (i.e., men and women) in reproductive health care, it should re-evaluate its discourse and practices.

References

Allen, B. (1995). "Diversity" and organizational communication. <u>Journal of Applied Communication Research, 23,</u> 143-155.

Cheney, G. (1983). On the various and changing meanings of organizational membership: A field study of organizational identification. <u>Communication Monographs, 50,</u> 342-362.

Eisenberg, E. (1984). Ambiguity as strategy in organizational communication. <u>Communication Monographs, 51,</u> 227-242.

Fairhurst, G., Jordan, J., & Neuwirth, K. (1997). Why are we here? Managing the meaning of an organizational mission statement. <u>Journal of Applied Communication Research, 25,</u> 243-263.

Planned Parenthood. (2001). Home page [online]. Planned Parenthood Federation of America, Inc. Available: http://www.plannedparenthood.org/ [2001, March 20th].

List of references goes on a separate page.

"References" is centered at the top of the page using upper and lower case letters. Double space to the first entry.

Observe the same margins and pagination requirements as the rest of the manuscript.

The first line of each entry is indented 1/2 inch or approximately five spaces. Each subsequent line is flush left.

Double space between: "References," within each entry and between each entry.

Note that in APA, the underlining of a title includes the punctuation at the end of the title.

APPENDIX C
Model Annotated Bibliography in <u>APA</u> Style

Media Use   1

Running head: LONELINESS AND MASS MEDIA USE

Loneliness and Mass Media Use: An Annotated Bibliography

Jane Doe

Southwest Missouri State University

Loneliness and Mass Media Use

Austin, A. (1984). Loneliness and the attributes of movie going. Psychological Reports, 55, 223-227.

This study examined how loneliness is related to various movie-going attributes. Four-hundred-and-eighty-three college students randomly selected from a Midwestern university ranging in ages from 16 to 36 years old participated. A questionnaire using the Revised UCLA Loneliness Scale, demographic items, and questions relating to movie going attendance was given to the students. The movie attendance questions asked about the pattern of movie attendance, whether they went on a regular basis or in streaks, how far in advance they made their decisions about going to the movies, and whether they went to the movies alone or in a group. Using the UCLA scale, three types of loneliness were defined: intimate (a feeling of isolation), social (a sense of not having a social network), and affiliation (the feeling of not belonging). The results showed no significant difference between the three types of loneliness and the pattern and frequency of movie going. There was a pattern discovered between the type of loneliness and the size of the group attending the movies. Those who had a feeling of "not belonging" attended movies in smaller groups. The overall results of the study suggested few differences between lonely and less lonely college students and movie-going patterns. According to this study loneliness did not bring about more regular movie attendance.

Center the title of the manuscript using upper and lower case letters. Double space to the first line of the manuscript.

Note that in APA, the underlining of a title includes the punctuation at the end of the title.

Indent each new paragraph 1/2 inch or approximately five spaces from the left margin.

The first line of each entry is indented 1/2 inch or approximately five spaces. Each subsequent line is flush left.

Austin, A. (1985). Loneliness and use of six mass media among college students. Psychological Reports, 56, 323-327.

Paginate every page of the manuscript; double space throughout.

This study examined the relationship between loneliness and mass media consumption among college students. Four-hundred-and-eighty-three college students ranging in age from 16 to 36 years old participated. The students were given a questionnaire containing the Revised UCLA Loneliness Scale, demographic questions and questions pertaining to their use of mass media, including television, movies, newspapers, magazines, radio and books (excluding textbooks). Overall, the results indicated little relationship between loneliness and frequency of media use. The authors concluded that students might use alternative methods to relieve loneliness other than increasing mass media consumption, which include the built in sociability of college life and the responsibilities associated with class work.

Elliott, W. & Quattlebaum, C. (1979). Similarities in patterns of media use. The Western Journal of speech Communication, 43, 61-92.

Observe one inch margins on all sides of the manuscript.

The purpose of this study was to determine the consequences of media use sought by media users. A questionnaire was developed which examined eight different media and the relative strength of the specific medium in relation to the individual's specific needs or reasons for using a specific media. The questionnaire should determine how eight media were used in the satisfaction of ten gratification items. Of the 259 subjects completing the questionnaires, males made up 61.2% of the sample and females 38.8%. Results indicate that two major patterns in media use are: (1) people use media as a means to maintain contact with society and (2) people use media to fulfill individual needs. The researchers concluded that television was the most generally satisfactory medium. Books, film, and recorded music showed parallel patterns of need satisfaction with one interpersonal medium, friends. Media appear to function differently in need satisfaction. Availability, cost, and involvement may also be factors in media differentiation.

Finn, S., & Gorr, M. (1988). Social isolation and social support as correlates of television motivations. Communication Research, 5, 135-158.

This study examined the relationship between motivations for television viewing and personality differences. The students were selected from the University of North Carolina over a three-year period. Approximately 96 students were selected each year to create a panel demographically similar to the undergraduate student population. Once a week, the students were interviewed and responded with yes/no answers into a computer. The students were asked questions pertaining to loneliness, shyness and interpersonal support as well as television viewing habits. The researchers divided motives into two headings with loneliness, shyness, habit, and companionship falling under the heading of "social compensation," and relaxation, entertainment, and arousal under "mood management." The hypothesis was students with strong social skills would react positively to viewing habits under "mood management" and those with weak social skills would react positively with "social compensation" viewing habits. The study supported their hypothesis. It also found that as level of social support increased, so did the level of television viewing for mood management.

Kubey, R. (1986). Television use in everyday life: coping with unstructured time. Journal of Communication, 36, 108-123.

The purpose of this study was to observe any relationships between subjective experience occurring in particular domains of daily life and an individual's level of television viewing. One hundred subjects (54% males, 63% females) employed full-time at five companies in the Chicago area participated in the study. Examination of the moods in which TV viewing is embedded should lead to greater success in establishing when and why people watch television. This study was conducted on site, not in the laboratory. These experiments employed experience sampling, a method that allows for the study of the total range of reportable moods, thoughts, and behaviors as they occur in normal daily experience. Each respondent carried a "pager" or "beeper." Subjects are "beeped" seven to nine times per day. After being signaled, each respondent filled out a Random Activity Information Sheet (RAIS) that asked questions concerning basic mood and activity. Results indicated particular kinds of experience (moods) occurring among certain kinds of people (e.g., less privileged and divorced and separated persons) and under certain conditions (solitary and un-structured time) could explain particular uses of media (heavy television viewing). When people from less affluent, less educated, less privileged, and divorced or separated demographic groups feel bad in unstructured or solitary situations and television is available, they are generally more inclined to watch than are more affluent, more educated, more privileged and married respondents. This study concluded that feeling bad in unstructured and solitary times leads to an increase use of television.

Lull, J. (1986). Social use of television. Human Communication Research, 6, 197-209.

This study explored the nature of social uses that audience members make of television. More than 200 families, representing blue-collar, white-collar, and farm types were studied. This study utilized a participant observational methodology (ethnography) as the means for data collection. The ethnographic methodology consisted of (1) participant observation, (2) the use of informants, and (3) in-depth interviewing. Observers looked for regularity in communicative acts reflected in interpersonal roles and relationships associated with the use of mass media. Social uses of television in the home are of two types: structural and relational. Two components of structural uses are environmental (background noise, companionship, entertainment) and regulative (punctuation of time and activity talk patterns). The associated components of the relational dimension are communication facilitation, affiliation/avoidance, social learning, competence/dominance. This study concluded that it may be very helpful to make inferences on the basis of the four major divisions of the relational dimension in order to rationalize specific "viewer types" or "family types." This may allow the individual to determine if a person or family uses television intentionally for the facilitation of effective family communication; for the potential to construct the desired degree of interpersonal affiliation; for learning about how to behave in the social world; or for demonstrating competence or dominating others in the viewer group.

Perloff, R., Quarles, R. & Drutz, M. (1988). Loneliness, depression and the use of television. Journalism Quarterly, 60, 353-356.

This study assessed the impact of the situational constraint of social isolation and depression on the uses of television by college students. One hundred and fifty urban university students ages 18-26 in an introductory mass communication course were surveyed. Respondents filled out a questionnaire including questions on dating, number of friends, dissatisfaction with relationships, and depression. They were also asked the extent to which they watched television to relieve boredom or to escape from problems. The results showed dating involvement only impacted television viewing due to the amount of free time the student had. Depression did not affect television time. Depression did have a modest impact on the viewer's involvement with television characters, but not the amount of television they watched. For television viewing time, subjective dispositions had a stronger impact than did situational variables, and situational variables affected the media variables indirectly through the dispositional variables.

Perse, E., & Rubin, A. (1990). Chronic loneliness and television use. Journal of Broadcasting & Electronic Media, 34, 37-53.

This article contains two studies investigating the relationship between chronic loneliness and television use. One study examined loneliness and local news viewing, the other loneliness and soap opera viewing. In the first study 380 non-traditional students enrolled in evening classes at a Midwest university completed a self-administered questionnaire. Twenty questions were from the UCLA Loneliness Scale to measure loneliness, the rest were viewing motive questions from previous research. The study found no substantial differences between the non-lonely and chronically lonely students in their media use, other than the chronic lonely tend to listen more to the radio. They also found lonely people watch news to pass the time rather than for informational or entertainment purposes. In the second study, 460 undergraduate students at a large Midwestern

university completed a self-administered questionnaire.
Three hundred and twenty-eight reported they watched soap
operas, with 68.9% being female. They were asked questions
from the UCLA Loneliness Scale to measure loneliness and
were asked questions about interpersonal channels and their
reasons for watching their favorite daytime soap operas.
Ninety-one percent of those identified as chronically lonely
watched television on a more regular basis. Sixty-three
percent of those identified as chronically lonely were less
involved in the soap operas compared to those who were
identified as not lonely. The conclusion was the chronically
lonely primarily use television to pass the time and don't
become involved in what they are watching. They do not use
the media as a substitute for social interaction.

Rubin, A., Perse, E. & Powell, R. (1985). Loneliness,
parasocial interaction, and local television news viewing.
Human Communication Research, 12, 155-180.

This study examined the relationship between loneliness
and the level of parasocial interactions. Hypotheses were
developed predicting parasocial interaction from both a social
interaction need due to loneliness and instrumental television
use. Questionnaires were completed by 329 persons (65%
females, 38% male). Questionnaires were administered during
class periods to 390 persons enrolled in 26 evening sections
on two regional campuses. A total of 339 respondents (86.9%)
indicated that they watched local television news. The
subjects' loneliness levels were measured with the revised
UCLA Loneliness Scale. Results indicated that loneliness and
interpersonal communication channel use are negatively
related. Loneliness and television reliance are positively
related. Ritualized news viewing to fill excess free time was
related to more television viewing. Conclusions were that

individuals linked psychological need to media use and its outcomes. Parasocial interaction can fulfill a social need for interaction and a major determinant of parasocial interaction is a function of an individual's level of loneliness. This study has developed a reliable empirical measure of parasocial interaction to measure feelings of audience relationships with local television news personalities.

Turow, J. (1974). Talk show radio as interpersonal communication. Journal of Broadcasting, 18, 171-179.

This study investigates the use of broadcasting as a substitute for traditional forms of interpersonal communication. This study was conducted at a Philadelphia-based radio station. Calls coming to the "talk jockey" were screened, allowing brief interviews with callers concerning their motives for calling, their attitudes towards society (as measured by the Strole Anomia Scale). Basic demographic information was also obtained. As a group, the callers appeared to be more geographically isolated and less mobile than the general population. Callers tended to be over 60 years of age and came from lower socio-economic class. A large number of the callers were chronically ill or invalids. The over-whelming majority of the callers welcome the interactive contact the talk show provided, along with the interactive dimension combined with the anonymity of the telephone. This study concluded that talk show radio callers are motivated to dial the station out of need for interpersonal contact rather than out of a desire to incite social reform.

APPENDIX D
Model Journal Critique in <u>APA</u> Style

Sex and Social Support   1

Running head: SEX AND SOCIAL SUPPORT

Sex Differences and Similarities in the Communication of

Social Support:

A Journal Article Critique

Michelle Redepenning

Minnesota State University Moorhead

In APA, pagination includes a short abbreviation of the title and the page number on every page of the manuscript, including the title page.

The running head only appears on the title page of the manuscript and is used by journal editors for publication purposes. Note the unusual use of upper and lower case letters. Students frequently make mistakes in typing the running head.

Include title, your first and last name, and your school affiliation, all double spaced using upper and lower case letters.

Sex and Social Support   2

Sex Differences and Similarities in the

Communication of Social Support:

A Journal Article Critique

<u>Source</u>

Goldsmith, D., & Dun, S. (1997). Sex differences and similarities in the communication of social support. <u>Journal of Social and Personal Relationships, 14</u>, 317-337.

<u>Purpose</u>

Previous research suggests that because men and women represent different cultures, they may respond differently when communicating support. According to such perspectives, men and women communicate differently in interpersonal relationships and such differences are consistent with instrumental versus expressive roles. Despite limited supporting evidence, these are widely accepted views in both public and academic discourse. The purpose of this study was to observe whether, in fact, differences exist in the communication of social support among men and women. To do this, the authors examined differences in length, frequency, and communication styles used by men and women in response to scenarios requiring the communication of social support.

<u>Rationale</u>

Ideologies about sex differences in the communication of social support are reflected and reinforced in the discourses of popular culture; yet, there is little empirical data upon which belief systems are based. The authors attempt to challenge the foundation upon which such assumptions rest. In addition to making theoretical contributions to existing literature on gender communication and social support, the project has practical value. Common assumptions that men only provide instrumental support and women only provide

---

Paginate every page of the manuscript.

Center the title of the manuscript using upper and lower case letters. Double space to the first line of the manuscript.

When citing the article you are critiquing, follow the rules for citing a source as it would appear in a list of Works Cited or References.

Do not use full justification, use a ragged right hand margin.

For most student papers you will use two types of headings: level 1 and level 2. Level 1 headings are centered in the page. Level 2 headings are flush to the left margin and underlined. Use upper and lower case letters for all headings. Do not use boldface. There are three level 2 headings on this page of the journal critique.

Indent the first line of each new paragraph 1/2 inch or approximately five spaces from the left margin.

Observe 1 inch margins on all sides of the manuscript.

emotional support, if inaccurate, may seriously limit

individuals' perceptions of their communication abilities and

choices. Additionally, even if males and females differ in the

amount of and type of support provided in relationships, both

genders can learn how to provide instrumental and

expressive support.

Methodology

The authors empirically tested ten hypotheses based on

previous research:

H1: Men's responses will be shorter than women's

responses;

H2: Men and women will not differ in the frequency of

responses that discuss actions to solve the problem or

alleviate negative emotions;

H3: Women's responses will discuss the other's problems

and emotional reactions more frequently than will men's

responses;

H4: Men will deny problems and emotions more often

than women;

H5: Men's responses will discuss actions more often than

problems or emotions;

H6: Women's responses will discuss problems and

emotions more often than actions;

H7: Men and women will exhibit different patterns of

relative frequency of talk about problems, emotions, and

actions;

H8: For men, denying problems and emotions will be

more common than other ways of talking about problems

and emotions;

H9: For women, denying problems and emotions will be

less common than other ways of talking about problems

and emotions; and

H10: Men and women will exhibit different patterns of relative frequency of denying or not denying problems and emotions.

One-hundred and nineteen undergraduates, 49 men and 51 women between the ages of 18 and 22 years, were asked to read and respond to nine situations in which another person disclosed some problem and appeared to be upset about that problem. Responses were tape-recorded and transcribed. To analyze the data, the authors used a coding system in which students' responses were categorized as problem-focused, emotion-focused, or action-focused.

Following the initial coding, authors analyzed problem and emotion-focused responses to determine "whether or not a speaker was verbally denying or minimizing a problem or emotional reaction" (p. 325). After coding of transcripts, the authors relied primarily on ANOVA procedures and t-tests, including follow-up procedures when appropriate, to test the hypotheses about gender differences in the communication of support.

Results

The results of the study found little support for past claims that men and women represent different cultures and therefore communicate differently when offering support. Consistent with H1, researchers found that women provided significantly longer responses than men. In addition, the length of responses did vary by situation. Researchers discovered a contradiction to H2 predicting that men and women will not differ in the amount of action-focused support. In fact, women's communication included significantly more action-focused responses than men. H3 was partially supported in that women's responses were significantly more emotion-focused than men's. Women and men did not differ in the number of problem-focused responses.

Since men and women differed in length of responses, researchers controlled for that difference in subsequent hypothesis-testing. Additional tests revealed that men and women did not differ in their responses in terms of emotion-focus or action- focus; however, men overwhelmingly focused their responses on the problem. H4 was partially supported as well indicating women and men differed significantly in the denial of the problem, but did not differ in the denial of emotions. H5 was supported that men provide more action focus than emotion focus responses. Surprisingly, both men and women frequently communicated both problem and action-focused responses more often than emotion focused responses.

Contrary to H8, Men were more likely to respond in ways that would not deny or minimize experiences rather than engage in the denial of a problem or emotion. Women were also more likely to talk about problems and emotions without denying them, thus supporting H9. Thus, contrary to H10, men and women were roughly similar in terms of not denying a problem or emotion in their communication of social support.

The overall conclusions suggest that there is little evidence in support of dominant stereotypes that women typically provide empathic emotional support and men typically provide instrumental advice and aid. In short, these results suggest that sex differences in the communication of social support are exceedingly small and the similarities between the sexes are substantial.

Evaluation

This study has broad theoretical scope in the sense that the results provide a base from which to question assumptions about gendered communication in general as well as the gendered communication of social support specifically. The authors challenge future researchers to focus on similarities across situations and genders as well as potential communication differences.

One potential weakness of this study is the sample of participants. First, the participants were not randomly selected. Additionally, the sample included mostly white, college students, between the ages of 18 and 22 years. Most participants were communication majors most likely educated in sex differences and gender stereotypes. I question whether the same data collection process would have yielded similar results with a more diverse population – an audience consisting of people with varying ages, races, religions, geographic locations, education levels and socioeconomic statuses. Future research designs would have more external validity if the sample was more diverse and participants were selected using more rigorous methods. The generalizability of the current results are limited by the sample.

A second potential weakness is the difficulty in receiving genuine and accurate feedback from respondents. Rather than analyzing the participants' verbal and non-verbal behaviors when engaged in naturally occurring dialogue, participants listened to hypothetical situations and shared their hypothetical responses with a tape recorder. It may be difficult to determine whether responses are consistent with how people would actually communicate in everyday situations requiring social support. Research designs would have more internal validity if they were to observe participants during

naturally occurring face-to-face encounters with a 'live'
person experiencing the need for social and/or emotional
support. Of course, it is difficult to obtain access to such
interactions for research purposes.

From a heuristic perspective, this study has merit.
Because mainstream culture perpetuates the ideology that
women communicate primarily emotional support and men
communicate primarily instrumental support, research that
provides alternative ways of thinking is critical to truly
understanding patterns of gendered communication. There
are also practical implications for a program of research on
the study of sex differences and similarities. Most self-help
books and other artifacts throughout our culture highlight
extreme gender differences and styles of communication.
Collectively, this discourse potentially influences not only
dominant perceptions of gender differences but also the way
in which men and women communicate with family, friends
and in the workplace. If indeed future research shows that
women and men communicate similarly when providing
support, such findings would have profound implications for
popular discourse on gender differences.

APPENDIX E
Model Research Report in <u>APA</u> Style

Lecture Cues   1

Running head: ORGANIZATIONAL LECTURE CUES

The Effects of Organizational Lecture Cues on Student

Notetaking

and Cognitive Learning

Harold W. Smith

Northern Central University

Russell D. Smith

Midwestern State University

In APA, pagination includes a short abbreviation of the title and the page number on every page of the manuscript, including the title page.

The running head only appears on the title page of the manuscript and is used by journal editors for publication purposes. Note the unusual use of upper and lower case letters. Students frequently make mistakes in typing the running head.

Include title, your first and last name, and your school affiliation, all double spaced using upper and lower case letters.

Abstract

This experimental study tested the effect of teachers' use of organizational lecture cues and students' (N = 60) notetaking on achievement. Results of the experiment indicated that (a) teacher organizational lecture cues and student notetaking each boosted achievement and (b) organizational cues and organization of students' notes are significant predictors of achievement. Based on these and other findings, it was concluded that teachers' use of organizational cues coupled with student notetaking results in greater student learning.

"Abstract" is centered at the top of the page in upper and lower case letters.

Note that the first word in the abstract is not indented 1/2 inch as are new paragraphs throughout the manuscript.

An abstract is a very concise statement that summarizes for the reader the content of the manuscript. Abstracts are most commonly associated with the reporting of empirical study and are not common for the typical student paper.

The Effects of Organizational Lecture Cues on Student

Notetaking and Cognitive Learning

A fact of life for many college students is that notetaking remains an essential ingredient for academic success. This fact is partly due to the observation that the lecture method remains a "sacred cow" among most college and university instructors (Carrier, Williams, & Dalagard, 1988). Because college instructors view lecturing as a central aspect of their professional identity, this format of instruction has become common throughout college and university classrooms, even in an era championing group-based and active learning teaching strategies (McKeachie, 1999). Although vernacular descriptions of the lecture situation assume students are merely passive receptors of knowledge, such descriptions may be overly pessimistic. In fact, students quickly learn that active listening behaviors, including taking notes, are required for success.

The problem with this lecture - notetaking relationship is twofold. First, not all students are equal in their notetaking skills. Although students believe that notetaking is both important and common in the college setting (Carrier et al., 1988; Palmatier & Bennett, 1974), they do not always take effective notes. In a lecture situation some students (using shorthand) seem to want to record everything said by the lecturer," observed Hartley and Davies (1978), "others pick and choose relevant points, and others indulge in a certain amount of doodling whilst they listen" (p. 207). This variance in notetaking skill (or effort) results in some students having more complete notes than others. In general, upper level students tend to take more notes than lower level

---

Paginate every page of the manuscript.
Center the title of the manuscript using upper and lower case letters. Double space to the first line of the manuscript.
Do not use full justification, use a ragged right hand margin.
Note the use of the ampersand sign "&" in the Carrier et. al. citation instead of "and." This is a distinguishing characteristic of APA style.
In the text of the paper use "and" not the ampersand.
Indent the first line of each new paragraph 1/2 inch or approximately five spaces from the left margin.
Observe 1 inch margins on all sides of the manuscript.

students (Kiewra, 1984). Moreover, research by Locke (1977) indicates that students record approximately 60% of the lecture points, and that students record more notes from material written on the board (88%) than material presented orally (52%). Other research has found that the amount of lecture information recorded by students is quite lower, somewhere between 30-40% (Kiewra, 1984).

A distinguishing characteristic of APA style is to include the date of publication or access in the in-text citation.

The problem of inadequate and varied skill in notetaking is compounded by the importance of notetaking on students' academic success. Several studies (Carrier et al., 1988; Kiewra, Benton, Kim, Risch, & Christensen, 1995; Kiewra et al., 1991a; Kiewra, Mayer, Christensen, Kim, & Risch, 1991b; Palmatier & Bennett, 1974; Rickards & Friedman, 1978) demonstrate that notetaking generally results in better student performance. The consistency of these findings leave little doubt that improving the notetaking effectiveness for students should be a central objective for applied instructional communication research.

"et al." is Latin for "and all."

When two or more citations from the same author have the same year of publication, you must include lower case letters (e.g., "a" and "b" to distinguish between the citations. Notice how this is used in the two Kiewra (1991) citations. In the list of references, alphabetize by author's last name to determine which citation is designated "a," which is "b" and so on.

Based on the rationale that notetaking effectiveness and consequently achievement, is influenced by the way lecture information is presented, the present study explored whether or not the use of explicit organizational cues in a lecture could increase students' notetaking effectiveness and achievement. The study consisted of a 2 x 2 experimental design where students either took notes or did not take notes over a lecture containing or not containing organizational cues. It was hypothesized that students taking notes over the lecture containing organizational cues would achieve at higher levels on recall tests and that students hearing the lecture with organizational cues would take qualitatively and quantitatively more effective notes.

Review of Literature

> For most student papers you will use two types of headings: level 1 and level 2. Level 1 headings are centered in the page. Level 2 headings are flush to the left margin and underlined. Use upper and lower case letters for all headings. Do not use boldface. "Review of Literature" is a level 1 heading.

Research exploring the importance of notetaking has found that both the quantity and quality of students' notes is important in terms of achievement. For example, Locke (1977) found that the number of ideas recorded in students' notes is positively related to recall of lecture information. Although the importance of recording a complete set of notes is intuitive, other aspects of notetaking (i.e., notetaking format) could also impact achievement. For instance, Kiewra and colleagues (1991a) found that using a matrix for notetaking was superior to conventional notetaking for immediate recall, and in another study, found that outline notetaking was superior to conventional notetaking in terms of both immediate and delayed recall (Kiewra et al., 1995). Evidence from other researchers indicate that notetaking combined with periodic summarization of main points from a lecture also boosts recall (Davis & Hult, 1997). Collectively, evidence on notetaking effectiveness leads to the conclusion that both the number of ideas recorded in students' notes (quantitative effectiveness) as well as the format of those ideas (qualitative effectiveness) are important elements of overall notetaking effectiveness and subsequent recall of information.

Given that notetaking effectiveness, both qualitative and quantitative, appears to impact achievement, how can teachers help students take better notes? Unfortunately, research in instructional communication provides little guidance in this area. Researchers in allied disciplines attempting to answer this question have explored various cuing techniques used during lecture situations that increase the quantity and quality of students' notes (for a review see Kiewra, 1991). For example, selection cues are strategies that help students pick out important elements from a lecture.

> APA style does not recommend for text features like bolding and italics. To emphasize text you should simply underline it.

Selection cues have been operationalized as conspicuous red or green cards to signal when notes should be recorded (Moore, 1968), writing information on the chalkboard (Locke, 1977) or providing other written signals (Frank, Garlinger, & Kiewra, 1989), use of skeletal outlines (Stencel, 1998), repetition of lectures (Kiewra et al., 1991b), and verbally stressing points by saying this is important (Scerbo, Warm, Dember, & Grasha, 1992). Each of the aforementioned selection cue strategies have been shown to increase the number of ideas recorded in students' notes.

Despite evidence that a variety of selection cues boost quantitative notetaking effectiveness, two salient questions remain unresolved. First, do these communication strategies increase the qualitative effectiveness of notes? Although the sheer quantity of ideas recorded in students' notes is undoubtedly related to achievement, the quality of those notes are also important. Currently, it is unclear whether or not cues used during a lecture has an effect on the qualitative effectiveness of notes. Second, at least some of the selection cues explored in previous research lack practical utility. Not all students have access to tapes of lectures, and consequently, repetition is not an option. Moreover, it is unlikely that many teachers will enthusiastically adopt the red card/green card strategy. Although we do not discount the utility of using importance cues, the chalkboard, or skeletal notes, our objective was to explore the utility of using another type of selection cue called organizational cues.

Organizational cues are verbal statements used by teachers to indicate the structural elements of a lecture. Such cues can include advance organizers, internal previews, internal summaries, and spoken numeric signposts of main and subordinate points. Although the effects of organizational cues in lectures have not been explicitly explored, two distinct programs of research suggest that these types of cues might improve students' notetaking and achievement.

Instructional communication researchers have consistently documented a connection between teacher immediacy and student learning. Although various theories have been used to explain this relationship, Kelley and Gorham (1988) speculate that immediacy cues increase students' attention to material. Although immediacy cues are distinct from organizational cues, Kelly and Gorham's rationale lends credibility to the argument that cues used during a lecture influence students' attention and learning. Other research in communication has found that the organization of information is also positively related to recall (Spicer & Bassett, 1976).

Although research in communication leads one to the conclusion that how teachers present information matters, research on cues used in expository text provides even more compelling evidence for the utility of organizational lecture cues. As explained by Lorch (1989), expository text includes a number of selection cues that signal readers about structural and content elements. Headings, titles, enumeration devices (e.g., numbering the points in an argument), and typographical characteristics are all examples of selection cues, or signals, found in text. Studies have found that organizational cues in text passages increase recall (Kardash & Noel, 2000; Myers, Pezdek, & Coulson, 1973), increase the quality of problem-solving solutions (Lockitch & Mayer, 1983), and decrease reliance on verbatim memory and primacy memory (Mayer, Cook, & Dyck, 1984). Although text signals boost achievement, questions remain whether these types of cues have a similar effect during lectures.

Based on the rationale provided in notetaking literature as well as literature on text signaling, several predictions were generated. First, previous research indicates that the cues provided during a lecture as well as student notetaking over a lecture improve student achievement. Consequently, it was predicted that students who took notes over the lecture containing organizational cues would learn more than students hearing lectures without cues and/or notetaking.

H1: Students who take notes over lectures containing organizational cues will score higher on achievement tests than students who do not take notes or hear lectures without organizational cues.

Furthermore, use of organizational cues could result in more effective notetaking because the cues make the organization of the lecture explicit. Thus, it was predicted that both the quantity and quality of students' notes would be greater in the cued condition than the uncued condition.

H2: Students who hear lectures with organizational cues will have qualitatively and quantitatively more effective notes than students who hear lectures without organizational cues.

Finally, previous research indicated that the completeness of students' notes is positively related to achievement. Because the organization of students' notes also potentially impacts their ability to store, organize, and retrieve information, it was predicted that both note completeness and note organization would be positively related to achievement.

H3: Student achievement is positively related to both note quantity and note organization.

> Double space text throughout the manuscript.

Method

Participants & Design

Note the use of a level 1 and level 2 heading for organizing the material.

Participants were 60 undergraduate students enrolled in a basic communication course at a large Midwestern public university. The basic communication course is required for most majors at the university, thus, participants were selected randomly from a potential sample representing a broad range of majors and academic backgrounds. There were slightly more females (n=31) than males (n=27; 2 did not report gender) and the participants' average age was 22.58 ($\underline{SD}$ = 4.85). In terms of class standing, 14 of the participants were Freshmen (23.3%), 11 were Sophomores (18.3%), 18 were Juniors (30%), and 17 were Seniors (28.3%). Participants indicated they had been in college for an average of 5.64 semesters ($\underline{SD}$ = 3.35) and had an average GPA of 2.95 ($\underline{SD}$ = .52). All participants received extra credit for participation and were informed of their rights as participants with standard informed consent procedures. Participants were randomly assigned to one cell of a 2 x 2 design where the first factor was lecture cues (explicit organizational cues were either present or absent) and the second factor was notetaking (students either recorded lecture notes or listened without taking notes).

In APA statistical notations are underlined.

Experimental Materials

Materials used for the experiment included two versions of a scripted, audio-taped lecture as well as two tests to measure students' recall of lecture content. The lecture was read by a female colleague not involved in the experiment and was audio-taped to control for possible nonverbal communication effects. The lecture material addressed 4 different theories about human communication processes (Coordinated Management of Meaning, Universal Audience, General Systems theory, and Media Bias theory) by describing 5 common topic areas for each theory (definition/description, its predominant context, examples illustrating the theory, how the theory explains potential mis-communication, and a specific application of the theory).

Because the lecture was scripted and taped, two versions of the lecture were created: a cued and un-cued version. The cued lecture contained explicit organizational cues which highlighted the structural organization of the lecture by drawing students' attention to the names and order of the theories and identified the 5 common topic areas. For example, the cued lecture contained these phrases: "The second context I will discuss is public communication" and, "Now I will present a theory for public communication." Students in the cued lecture also heard an advance organizer in the introduction of the lecture. The advance organizer was worded in this way:

> This lesson describes four communication theories: coordinated management of meaning theory, universal audience theory, general systems theory, and media bias theory. For each of these theories, we consider five things: First, I will provide a description of the theory. Second, we discuss the communication context associated with the theory. Third, I will discuss how the theory helps us understand miscommunication in that context. Fourth we will learn about an example of the theory. Finally, we consider how the theory can be applied to our understanding of communication.

This is a block quotation of forty words or more. Indent the entire quotation 1/2 inch or approximately five spaces from the left margin. Note that the quotation is double spaced like the rest of the text.

The cued version of the lecture contained 3, 045 words and lasted approximately 15 minutes.

Students hearing the un-cued lecture heard the same information as students hearing the cued lecture, however, explicit organizational cues were omitted. For instance, information on Universal Audience theory was presented in this way: "Another theory is Universal Audience theory which can be described as. . . ." Students hearing this lecture heard the following statements rather than an advance organizer:

In this lesson we consider several communication theories associated with several of the most common human communication contexts. To explain these, we will learn a lot of information, and after hearing it, you will have a much better understanding of what human communication is and how theories can help us understand how human communication works in a variety of situations and settings.

This version of the lecture contained 2, 997 words and lasted just over 13 minutes.

In addition to the lectures, two achievement tests were constructed to assess students' recall from the lectures. The first achievement test, called the structure test, asked students to recall the lecture framework including main topics (e.g., media bias theory, coordinated management of meaning theory, etc.) and sub-topics (e.g., definition, example, application, etc.). This test measured students' ability to recall and construct the lecture's organization independent of specific facts or examples. There were a possible 24 points on this test. The second test, called the detail test, presented the organizational framework of the lecture and asked students to provide associated details. For example, students were asked to write the definition, associated context, example, explanation of miscommunication, and application for general systems theory. This test assessed students' ability to recall specific facts and details from the lecture relative to their superordinate topics. Because there were 5 sub-topics covered for each theory, there were 20 possible points on this test.

Experimental Procedure

Students were randomly assigned to one of four rooms representing either the cued or un-cued and either the notes or no-notes conditions. All students were provided verbal instructions that they would listen to and be quizzed over a lecture on communication theory. After listening to the lecture, all participants were given 5 minutes to review the information. Students in the notes condition were instructed to review their notes but were asked to put them away after the review period. Students in the no notes condition were told to mentally review the information they had heard. After the review period, all participants were administered the two achievement tests and were instructed that they could not look ahead or backwards in the test packet nor could they go back and change answers. All students completed the tests in 15 minutes or less. The experimental procedure including listening to the lecture, reviewing the information, and taking the tests lasted approximately 45 minutes.

Scoring and Analysis

Scoring of the achievement tests involved awarding one point for each structural element (structure test) and detail (detail test) recorded by students. In addition to analyzing students' achievement on the two tests, students' notes were analyzed for organization and completeness. Students' note organization was assessed by determining whether the names of the four communication theories and five corresponding categories (per theory) were present in notes. Thus, note organization scores could range from 0 to 24. Students' note completeness was assessed by counting the number of details contained in notes. The scores recorded for note completeness could range from 0 to 20.

After constructing a scoring/coding manual for the tests and students' notes, one of the researchers and a colleague not involved in the study independently scored five sets of materials. After this initial scoring session, the two compared their scores for the materials and discussed differences so that reliability on subsequent scoring could be increased. This procedure resulted in overall reliability estimates of .93 for the structure test, .96 for the detail test, .90 for note organization, and .87 for note details. The scores from the two coders were averaged so that each student had one score for each of the tests and measures of notetaking effectiveness.

Data were analyzed using SPSS for windows; alpha was set at .05 for all statistical tests. To protect from type I error, a multivariate analysis of variance procedure was used to test for mean differences among treatment groups on each of the achievement tests. Univariate t-tests were used to test for mean differences in note completeness and organization based on the organizational cues factor. Finally regression procedures were used to determine how much variance in students' scores on the three achievement tests could be accounted for by the teachers' use of organizational cues, note organization, and note completeness.

Results

Results of the statistical tests supported the predictions guiding the study. Students who heard the lectures with organizational cues scored higher on the achievement tests than students who heard the lecture without cues. The combination of taking notes over the cued lectures resulted in the highest achievement levels whereas not taking notes and hearing the uncued lecture resulted in the lowest. Moreover, students who heard the lectures with cues recorded more structural elements and details from the lectures in their notes than their peers who heard the lectures without cues.

Achievement Tests

Multivariate analysis of variance procedures were used to test for mean differences between each of the four groups in terms of scores on each of the two achievement tests. The multivariate tests showed significant main effects for both the notetaking factor, Wilks' $\lambda = .79$, $\underline{F} = 7.32$ (2, 55), $\underline{p}.<.05$, $\eta^2 = .21$, and the cues factor, Wilks' $\lambda = .73$, $\underline{F} = 9.10$ (2, 54), $\underline{p}.<.05$, $\eta^2 = .27$. A significant Cues x Notes interaction was also detected, Wilks' $\lambda = .47$, $\underline{F} = 31.35$ (2, 55), $\underline{p}.<.05$, $\eta^2 = .53$.

With respect to the structure test, including explicit organizational cues in the lecture and having students take notes each resulted in higher scores. Significant main effects were found for both cuing, $\underline{F} = 52.17$ (1, 56), $\underline{p}. <.05$, $\eta^2 = .48$, and notetaking, $\underline{F} = 5.06$ (1, 56), $\underline{p}. <.05$, $\eta^2 = .08$. The interaction between cues and notetaking was not significant, $\underline{F} = 1.99$ (1, 56), $\underline{p}. >.05$, $\eta^2 = .03$. In terms of the detail test, a combination of notetaking and lecture cuing resulted in higher scores for students. Conversely, absence of cuing and/or notetaking resulted in substantially lower scores on this test. As with the lecture organization test, significant main effects were found for both cuing, $\underline{F} = 20.96$ (1, 56), $\underline{p}. <.05$, $\eta^2 = .27$, and notetaking, $\underline{F} = 12.03$ (1, 56), $\underline{p}. <.05$, $\eta^2 = .18$. Organizational cues and notetaking accounted for 27% and 18% of the variance in students' ability to recall lecture details, respectively. There was also a significant interaction between notetaking and cues for the detail test, $\underline{F} = 15.70$ (1, 56), $\underline{p}. <.05$, $\eta^2 = .22$. As indicated by comparisons of simple effects, students who heard the lecture with explicit organizational cues and took notes scored significantly higher on this test than students who did not take notes or who took notes and heard the un-cued lecture. Thus, the combination of cuing and notetaking resulted in higher achievement.

Notetaking

Initially, correlations were calculated to determine the statistical relationships between students' notetaking and achievement. In general, correlations revealed significant and positive relationships between the two measures of notetaking effectiveness and students' scores on the two achievement tests. As indicated by the coefficients, both the quantity and quality of students' notes are strongly correlated with achievement. To further explore these relationships, regression analyses were calculated for each test with note organization, note completeness, and use of organizational cues entered as predictor variables. Because results of the ANOVA procedures suggested that organizational cues should account for significant variance in students' scores, this factor was entered first and students' note completeness and organization was entered in a second block. The combination of all three predictor variables accounted for 54% of the variance in students' scores on the organization test, and 59% of the variance on the details test. As indicated by the coefficients, use of organizational cues was the only significant predictor of students' scores on the organization test and the organization of students' notes was the only significant predictor of scores on the detail test.

Students' notes were also analyzed to determine whether there were significant differences in students' note organization and note completeness depending on whether they heard the lecture with or without organizational cues. In general, the use of cues dramatically improved students' notes. Not only did students hearing the lecture with organizational cues record more structural elements of the lecture, but they also recorded more details. Tests of mean differences indicated significant differences for note organization, $t = 6.36$, $p < .05$, and note completeness, $t = 6.30$, $p < .05$. Students hearing the lecture with organizational cues recorded 54% ($M = 12.89$; $SD = 5.13$) of the organizational points and 64% ($M = 12.78$; $SD = 3.69$) of the lecture details whereas students hearing the lecture not containing cues only recorded 15% ($M = 3.58$; $SD = 2.70$) of the organizational points and 29% ($M = 5.87$; $SD = 2.29$) of the lecture details, respectively. In practical terms, students hearing the lecture containing explicit cues recorded nearly four times as many structural points and over twice as many details as students hearing the lecture without these explicit cues.

Discussion

The purpose of this study was to assess the effectiveness of using organizational lecture cues to increase students' quantitative notetaking effectiveness, qualitative notetaking effectiveness, and achievement. It was predicted that students taking notes over the lecture with organizational cues would score higher on the achievement tests than students not taking notes or not hearing the lecture with cues. It was also predicted that students' notes in the cued lectures would contain more details and would be more organized than students' notes in the un-cued lecture. Results of the study supported both of these predictions.

Based upon results of the experiment, three major findings are discussed. First, this study re-confirmed the previous finding that notetaking is strongly related to achievement (see Kiewra, 1984; Kiewra et al., 1985; Locke, 1977). In addition to the importance of note quantity, this study yielded new information concerning the importance of note quality as assessed through organization. Results indicated that when students record the organization of a lecture in their notes they were more likely to remember specific details from the lecture. Although previous literature has documented the relationship between note completeness and achievement (see Locke, 1977), findings of the current study suggest that recording structural elements of a lecture is perhaps more important. Notably, the organization of students' notes was the only significant predictor of students' recall on the detail test.

Second, this study found strong support for the use of organizational lecture cues because of the impact they had on student notetaking and achievement. Students hearing lectures with organizational cues recorded twice as many lecture details and nearly four times as many organizational points as those students hearing the lecture without organizational cues. The importance of this finding is underscored when placed in the context of the previous finding: When teachers use organizational cues in lectures students record more organized notes and when students record organized notes, their achievement dramatically increases. In practical terms, one would expect that students will learn a great deal more when teachers use organizational cues when presenting material. In fact, this was demonstrated on the achievement tests where organizational cues had effect sizes of .48 for the structure test and .27 for the detail test, respectively.

The final finding of this study related to a potential interaction between a teacher's use of organizational lecture cues and student notetaking. Although a significant Cues x Notetaking interaction was only found on the detail test, this interaction pattern was consistent on the structure tests and a significant multivariate interaction was also observed. Moreover, power for the interaction term on the structure test was low (.23), which raises the possibility that a significant interaction would not have been detected. In short, students benefited most when they took notes and heard organizational lecture cues. Alternatively, students who did not take notes and/or did not hear organizational lecture cues performed more poorly. Consequently, we suggest teachers use organizational cues because this strategy is cheap, easy, and has a potentially dramatic impact on student learning.

Although this study has important pragmatic and theoretical implications, additional research is warranted. For instance, future research should explore the effects of organizational lecture cues in a more naturalistic setting. The audio-taped lectures used in this study, while useful for controlling confounding variables, may lack external generalizability. Moreover, additional research efforts should explore how these teaching and learning behaviors vary depending on whether the type of material being taught is declarative, procedural or conceptual. For instance, would the importance of organizational clarity be magnified in situations where processes or behaviors are being taught? Finally, future studies should explore how organizational cues and notetaking impact learning among students with differing learning style preferences.

In conclusion, this study has explored the effects of teacher organizational clarity and student notetaking on cognitive learning. Results indicated that both teacher and student communication behaviors are critical elements in the classroom. In this study, students learned more when they took notes and when the teacher presented explicit organizational cues. It is advisable for teachers and students both to enact these behaviors because of their ease and the substantial effect they have on learning.

References

Carrier, C., Williams, M., & Dalagard, B. (1988). College students' perceptions of notetaking and their relationship to selected learner characteristics and course achievement. Research in Higher Education, 28, 223-239.

Davis, M., & Hult, R. (1997). Effects of writing summaries as a generative learning activity during notetaking. Teaching of Psychology, 24, 47-49.

Frank, B., Garlinger, D., & Kiewra, K. (1989). Use of embedded headings and intact outline with videotaped instruction. Journal of Educational Research, 82, 277-281.

Hartely, T., & Davies, I. (1978). Note-taking: A critical review. Programmed Learning and Educational Technology, 15, 207-224.

Kardash, C., & Noel, K. (2000). How organizational signals, need for cognition, and verbal ability affect text recall and recognition. Contemporary Educational Psychology, 25, 317-331.

Kelley, D., & Gorham, J. (1988). Effects of immediacy on recall of information. Communication Education, 37, 198-207.

Kiewra, K. (1984). Acquiring effective notetaking skills: An alternative to professional notetaking. Journal of Reading, 27, 299-301.

Kiewra, K. (1991). Aids to lecture learning. Educational Psychologist, 26, 37-53.

Kiewra, K., Benton, S., Kim, S., Risch, N., & Christensen, M. (1995). Effects of note-taking format and study technique on recall and relational performance. Contemporary Educational Psychology, 20, 172-187.

Observe the same margins and pagination requirements as the rest of the manuscript.

"References" is centered at the top of the page using upper and lower case letters. Double space to the first entry.

The first line of each entry is indented 1/2 inch or approximately five spaces. Each subsequent line is flush left.

List of references goes on a separate page.

Double space between: "References," within each entry and between each entry.

Kiewra, K., DuBois, N., Christain, D., McShane, A., Meyerhoffer, M., & Roskelley, D. (1991a). Note-taking functions and techniques. Journal of Educational Psychology, 83, 240-245.

Kiewra, K., Mayer, R., Christensen, M., Kim, S., & Risch, N. (1991b). Effects of repetition on recall and note-taking: Strategies for learning from lectures. Journal of Educational Psychology, 83, 120-123.

Locke, E. (1977). An empirical study of lecture note taking among college students. The Journal of Educational Research, 77, 93-99.

Lockitch, N., & Mayer, R. (1983). Signaling techniques that increase the understandability of expository prose. Journal of Educational Psychology, 75, 402-412.

Lorch, R. (1989). Text-signaling devices and their effects on reading and memory processes. Educational Psychology Review, 1, 209-234.

Mayer, R., Cook, L., & Dyck, J. (1984). Techniques that help readers build mental models from scientific text: Definitions pretraining and signaling. Journal of Educational Psychology, 76, 1089-1105.

McKeachie, W. (1999). Teaching tips: Strategies, research, and theory for college and university teachers. (10th ed.). New York: Houghton Mifflin Company.

Moore, J. (1968). Cuing for selective notetaking. Journal of Experimental Education, 36, 69-72.

Myers, J., Pezdek, K., & Coulson, D. (1973). Effect of prose organization upon free recall. Journal of Educational Psychology, 65, 313-320.

Palmatier, R., & Bennett, J. (1974). Notetaking habits of college students. Journal of Reading, 18, 215-218.

When lower-case letters are used in text citations to distinguish references, those letters must also appear in the reference citation. Notice the various Kiewra (1991) entries in this reference section. In the first entry no co-authors are listed and the years of publication are different. Consequently, no letter is needed. In the other entries the number of co-authors would result in the in-text citations appearing as "Kiewra et al., 1991. Lower case letters are required to indicate which citation is being referenced. By alphabetizing authors' last names you can determine which citation should be designated as "a," "b" and so forth.

Rickards, J., & Friedman, F. (1978). The encoding versus the external storage hypothesis in note taking. <u>Contemporary Educational Psychology, 3</u>, 136-143.

Scerbo, M., Warm, J., Dember, W., & Grasha, A. (1992). The role of time and cuing in a college lecture. <u>Contemporary Educational Psychology, 17</u>, 312-328.

Spicer, C., & Bassett, R. (1976). The effect of organization on learning from an informative message. <u>The Southern Communication Journal, 41</u>, 290-299.

Stencel, J. (1998). An interactive lecture notebook: Twelve ways to improve students' grades. <u>Journal of College Science Teaching, 27</u>, 343-345.

APPENDIX F
Model Speaking Preparation Outline
Following <u>APA</u> Guidelines

Kip Johnson
Dr. Scott Titsworth
Speech 101
April 13, 2001

An Informative Speech on Cell Phones

Specific Purpose: To inform my audience about the advantages
and disadvantages of cellular phones.

Central Idea: Cellular phones have several advantages and
disadvantages as a mobile communication device, a health and
safety tool, and a new opportunity for e-commerce.

Introduction

I.   Think fast! You are working at your job and you start to go
      into labor. Or, imagine that you are driving home at night
      and your car stalls while it is below zero. Or, you are
      driving down the street and see a person being robbed on
      the sidewalk. What do you do? You could be like Keaneau
      Reeves and take things into your own hands, or you could
      do what most sane people would do and make a call on your
      cell phone. But, we have all probably witnessed the dark
      side of cell phones. While watching Speed in the theatre,
      your movie experience could likely be interrupted by a cell
      phone call to an inconsiderate moviegoer.
II.   Cell phones are becoming an increasingly common element
      of our culture. Jorgen Bach, a professor from a university
      in Denmark, told Time Magazine that an estimated 500
      million people worldwide use cell phones, with 100 million
      of those being in the US (Ressner, Sautter, Thomas &
      Thompson, 2001).
III. I have owned a cell phone for nearly 2 years. Because I am
      worried about risks but also exited about the convenience of
      cell phones, I decided to investigate the benefits and risks of
      cell phones.
VI.   I intend to inform you about cell phones so that you can
      make a decision on whether you would want one.
      A. In my speech I will inform you about the benefits and
         dangers of cell phones.
      B. I specifically address the following points:
         1. The benefits and risks of cell phones as a mobile
            communication device.
         2. The benefits and risks of cell phones for health.
         3. The benefits and risks of cell phones for e-commerce.

(Transition: We all know that the primary use of cell phones is
for communication. In my first point I look at the uses of this
communication tool as well as some dangers it poses.)

Single space the
text of the outline.
Double space
between the major
sections of the
outline. This is done
to conserve length.

Note that "Specific
Purpose" and
"Central Idea" are
capitalized.

Introduction is a
major section of the
outline. Center
using upper and
lower case letters.
No bolding.

Many authors of
public speaking
texts allow you to
write out the
introduction and
conclusion of the
speech.

Body ———

> Center title of major sections like "Body."

I. Cell phones are popular tools for mobile communication.
   A. Cell phones make communication easy and convenient.
      1. Personal example of working on a farm and using cell phones while in the field.
      2. Personal example of using my cell phone while driving to school.
      3. Approximately 85% of those who own cell phones use them while driving, according to the National Conference of State Legislators (National Conference of State Legislators, 1999).
   B. Although cell phones are convenient, they also pose a danger if not used properly.
      1. A study reported in the New England Journal of Medicine found that use of cell phones quadrupled the risk of an automobile accident (National Conference of State Legislators, 1999).
        a. This is equal to the impairment caused by legal intoxication.
        b. The use of hands free devices does not appear to reduce the risk.
      2. Kaz Zielinski, a program manager for a company called Advanced Driver Training Services, explains that the act of using a cell phone simply distracts drivers (Zielinski, 2000).
        a. Dialing the phone causes you to look down.
        b. Talking on the phone can cause you to lose focus on objects, distance, etc.
        c. A ringing phone can startle you.
        d. Holding a phone reduces your ability to control the vehicle.

> Start re-numbering with Roman numeral "I" when you begin a new section of the outline.

> Note the rule of twos. You can't divide an idea into one part. For every Roman numeral I there is a II; for every A there is a B; for every 1 there is a 2; for every a there is a b.

(Transition: Now that we know that cell phones are a convenient, but potentially dangerous communication device, let's explore the impact of cell phones on health.)

II. Cell phones are useful tools for health and safety, but pose some risks.
   A. Cell phones have benefits for health.
      1. Cell phones improve the response time in emergencies.
      2. Cell phones are used to help women.
        a. The Wireless Foundation Home Page (2001) describes a program where women at risk of domestic violence are given free cell phones with airtime to stay in touch with their crisis counselors.
        b. To date, over 30,606 cell phones have been given out through this program.

> Transitional statements are written as complete sentences and appear in parentheses. Also note the double spacing that sets off the transitional statement from the rest of the outline.

B. Even though cell phones help people, there is some question regarding potential health risks.
   1. Some studies show that the radiation from cell phones can be linked to brain cancer (Ressner et al., 2001).
   2. The evidence on this potential risk is not conclusive. A recent study in the Journal of the American Medical Association and another in the New England Journal of Medicine found no statistical link between cell phone use and cancer risk (Ressner et al., 2001).
   3. Cell phone companies are starting to indicate an SAR rating on cell phone literature. The rule of thumb is that a lower SAR rating (say around .22) is safer than a higher one (around 1.6).

(Transition: The final area we will look at is the use of cell phones in e-commerce.)

III. Cell phones are becoming an important tool for e-commerce.
   A. We know that cell phones make business more convenient.
      1. Business executives use cell phones to make calling convenient.
      2. Consumers are increasingly using cell phones.
         a. Cell phones are already used for basic e-commerce like purchasing news and information services, checking current stock prices, and purchasing simple things like tickets (Bethoney, 2001).
         b. A news article in the E-Commerce Times also noted that corporations like Microsoft and RealNetworks will soon start selling multimedia content like movies and videos that can be played on new-generation multimedia capable cell phones (Hillebrand, 2000).
   B. Although cell phones will undoubtedly become an important tool for e-commerce, there is some danger depending on what the tool is used for.
      1. A recent article in Time indicated that cell phones could be used to gamble (Schenker, 2001).
         a. Predictions estimate that on-line gambling will jump from $3 billion in 2000 to $58 billion by 2004.
         b. A global poll by a Swedish mobile phone maker found that cell phones will make the betting impulse easier.
      2. Using cell phones for gambling is just like throwing money away at the casino, only easier.

Conclusion

(Transition: Now that you have learned about some benefits and dangers of cell phones, I hope you can make an informed choice on whether to get one.)

I.   In this speech I have presented you with several facts and examples of how cell phones are good and bad.
    A. Cell phones are excellent mobile communication tools, but they pose a danger for drivers.
    B. Cell phones make us safer in emergencies, but some claim they might expose us to dangerous radiation.
    C. Cell phones are new tools for e-commerce, but they also might make it easier to lose money on impulse decisions to buy or gamble.
II.   If you are driving around town and see a robbery taking place, using a cell phone is probably the best thing you could do. But, during those other times when life is not so exciting, keep in mind the dangers of using your cell phone.

References

Bethoney, H. (2001, January 15). Let your cell phone do the e-shopping [electronic]. eWeek, p. 75. Available: Expanded Academic Index.

Hillebrand, M. (2000, June 29). Internet video head for cell phones [on-line]. E-Commerce Times website. Available: htp://ecommercetimes.com [2000, March 21].

National Conference of State Legislators. (1999). Do any states restrict the use of cell phones in motor vehicles? State Legislatures, 25, 2.

Ressner, J., Sautter, U., Thomas, C. & Thompson, D. (2001, January 22). Buzzing about safety: The latest studies say there is no cell phone risk, but many users are making their own decisions about taking precautions. Time, pp. 48-52.

Schenker, J. L. (2001, January 22). Place your mobile bets: Gambling could be the killer application that will make third-generation cell phone licenses pay off. Time, pp. 46-48.

The Wireless Foundation. (No date). Call to protect home page [on-line]. In The Wireless Foundation Home Page. Available: http://www.wirelessfoundation.org [2001, March 21].

Zielinski, K. (2000). Cell phones and driving: A dangerous mix [electronic]? Risk & Insurance, 11, 17-18. Available: Expanded Academic Index.

Observe the same margins and pagination requirements as the rest of the manuscript.

"References" is centered at the top of the page using upper and lower case letters. Double space to the first entry.

The first line of each entry is indented 1/2 inch or approximately five spaces. Each subsequent line is flush left.

List of references goes on a separate page.

Double space between: "References," within each entry and between each entry.

APPENDIX G
Model Speaking Preparation Outline
Following <u>MLA</u> Guidelines

Mary Jane
Ms. Sandra House
Public Speaking 115
18 November 2002

Include your name, instructor's name, course number, course title and date. Single space the head flush left. Note the date format in MLA is Day/Month/Year.

Purchasing a Thanksgiving Turkey

Specific Purpose: To inform my audience of the factors to consider when purchasing a Thanksgiving turkey.

Center the title of the speech using upper and lower case letters.

Central Idea: When selecting a Thanksgiving turkey, the informed consumer should consider four factors: the size, the grade, the age, and whether the turkey is fresh or frozen.

Introduction

Note that "Specific Purpose" and "Central Idea" are capitalized.

I. How many of you are planning on having <u>Melegris gallopavo</u> for dinner in eight days? Well, this month on its Thanksgiving homepage, Butterball predicted that not only will ninety percent of all Americans enjoy a tasty meat of <u>Melegris Gallopavo</u> next Thursday, all together, we will consume a total of five hundred and thirty-five million pounds of it. If you haven't guessed already, <u>Melegris Gallopavo</u> is the scientific name for turkey.

Many authors of public speaking texts allow you to write out your introduction and conclusion.

II. With so many of us honoring the three hundred-year-old tradition of turkey for Thanksgiving, it is important for us to know the details we need to consider when we buy our turkeys. These factors are the size of the turkey, the meat grade of the turkey, the age of the turkey, and whether the turkey is fresh or frozen.

Body

Single space the text of the outline. Double space between the major sections of the outline: Title, specific purpose, central idea statement, introduction, body, conclusion and transitional statements. This is done to conserve space.

I. Size is the most important factor to consider when purchasing a turkey.
    A. Buying the right size turkey is important because you need enough of feed all your guests without having too much leftover.
    B. Not everyone agrees on the formula you should use to determine the size of turkey you want.
        1. On this month's Thanksgiving web page, Norbest, the world's third largest turkey company, says that you should buy three-fourths pound per person.
        2. Butterball on its web page suggests you calculate one and one half pounds per person.
        3. However, honeysuckle white recommends one pound per person.
        4. I would use one pound per person to figure the size because it is easier.
    C. The size is almost always written on the tag attached to the neck of the bird.

Note that the indention is consistent throughout at 1/2 inch. Also note that all of the symbols are aligned. Main points A, B and C are aligned. Subpoints 1, 2, 3 and 4 are aligned.

The preparation outline is written in complete sentences.

136

(Transition: After determining how large your Thanksgiving feast needs to be, the next major decision you need to make is the quality of the bird.)

II. What does the grade on the meat really mean?
   A. In their 1995 meat grading pamphlet, the Agriculture Marketing Service of the USDA says meat grading is a common language between producers and consumers.
   B. Grading is voluntary but according to the Nation Turkey Federation on its 1997 homepage, seventy percent of all turkeys are USDA graded.
   C. The USDA assigns the letters A, B, and C to poultry meat depending on its quality.
      1. You should always buy Grade A meat.
      2. In 1995 the USDA reported that to be considered Grade A the meat must exhibit four things.
         a. It must have a normal shape and no missing parts.
         b. It must be free of all broken bones.
         c. It must have well-distributed fat.
         d. It must be free of all feathers and discoloration.
      3. The grade of the meat is always displayed somewhere on the packaging around the turkey.

(Transition: Once you know how large a turkey you need and what quality to look for, you need to know the age of the bird you are buying.)

III. You need to know the approximate age of the bird before you buy the turkey.
   A. Turkeys are classified as either old or young.
      1. Old birds are referred to as mature, yearling, or just old.
      2. Young birds are referred to as young or fryer-roaster.
   B. You should always buy young because it is more tender.

(Transition: The last major decision to make is whether you want to purchase a fresh or frozen bird.)

IV. Finally, you must decide whether you want a frozen or fresh turkey.
   A. The first thing to consider when deciding is how much preparation time you have.
      1. Fresh turkeys do not need to be thawed, but you shouldn't buy it too far in advance.
      2. Frozen turkeys can be bought months in advance, but need days to thaw.
   B. The second thing to consider is that fresh turkeys tend to be more tender.

Pagination appears on every page of the preparation outline. Pagination in MLA includes your last time, two spaces and the page number 1/2 inch from the top and right margin.

Again note the common system of indentation and symbol alignment throughout the outline.

Note the rule of twos. You can't divide an idea into one part. For every Roman numeral I there is a II; for every A there is a B; for every 1 there is a 2; for every a there is a b.

Transitional statements are written as complete sentences and appear in parentheses. Also note the double spacing that sets off the transitional statement from the rest of the outline.

Jane 2

Conclusion

Now you've heard enough on purchasing a Thanksgiving turkey
to make an informed decision about the turkey you want to buy
whether it is a Butterball, Norbest, Honeysuckle white, or some
other brand of whole turkey. However, I advise you, next
Thursday when you are enjoying the time honored tradition of
<u>Mellegris Gallopavo</u> for Thanksgiving dinner, try not to think of
its size, grade, age, or whether it was frozen or fresh from the
store, just enjoy the taste.

Jane 2

Works Cited

Butterball Turkey Company. "How to Prepare a Picture-

Perfect Turkey." http://www.butterball.com (11 November 1999).

Honeysuckle white. "All about Turkey."

http://www.honeysucklewhite.com/html/whole_turkey.html (11

November 1999).

The National Turkey Federation. "The Turkey Food Service

Manual." http://www.turkeyfed.org/toc.html (16 November 1999).

Norbest Incorporated. "Talk'in Turkey Dinner."

http://www.norbest.com (11 November 1999).

United States Department of Agriculture. Agricultural

Marketing Service. "How to Buy Poultry." Washington, D.C.:

Government Printing Office, 1995.

United States Department of Agriculture. Agricultural

Marketing Service. "Meat Grinding and Certification Service."

Washington, D.C.: Government Printing Office, 1999.

The Works Cited is a separate page of the preparation outline as required by MLA.

"Works Cited" is centered at the top of the page using upper and lower case letters. Double space to the first entry.

Observe the same margins and pagination requirements as the rest of the preparation outline – 1/2 inch on all sides.

The first line of each entry is flush with the left margin; subsequent lines are indented 1/2 inch or approximately five spaces.

List the sources you cite in your preparation outline in alphabetical order following MLA guidelines for constructing a Works Cited page.

APPENDIX H
Student Exercises

Your Name: _____   Date _____

Chapter 3 Exercise 1

Chapter 3 discussed several issues related to common written assignments
in communication courses. Below are several terms and concepts from the
chapter. For each term/concept, provide a brief definition/explanation based
on what you read.

1. Full Content Outline:

2. Speaking Outline:

3. Internal Source Reference:

4. Bibliographic Source reference:

5. External Validity:

6. Internal Validity:

7. Negative Rationale:

8. Positive Rationale:

Your Name: _____ Date _____

Chapter 3 Exercise 2

Based on information presented in chapter 3, answer the following questions
by writing the best answer in the space provided. For each question, write
"T" for true or "F" for false. After indicating whether it is true or false, briefly
explain why.

_____ 1. Internal source references for a full content/preparation outline are
included in the list of references or works cited.

_____ 2. Bibliographic references on a full content/preparation outline are listed
alphabetically.

_____ 3. Speaking outlines are typically 2 to 4 pages in length.

_____ 4. If the last point in your introduction is identified with the Roman
numeral III, the first point in the body of your outline should be
identified with the Roman numeral IV.

_____ 5. The Works Cited page (MLA) or References page (APA) for your
outline should use Roman numerals to identify separate sources used
in the outline.

_____ 6. Full content/preparation outlines should be written using complete
sentences.

_____ 7. Sub-sub-points (designated with regular numbers like "2") should be
indented 5 spaces, or one tab, from the left margin of the outline.

Your Name: _____ Date _____

Chapter 3 Exercise 3

Chapter 3 discussed several criteria that can be used to evaluate empirical and/or humanistic research studies. For each criterion below, provide a brief definition/explanation based on what you read.

Theoretical Scope:

Appropriateness of Methodology:

Validity:

Heuristic Value:

Parsimony:

Your Name: _____   Date _____

Chapter 3 Exercise 4

Chapter 3 discusses how various writing assignments common in communication courses should be prepared. The section on composing a literature review suggests that literature reviews should be "mapped out" to determine how topics should be organized. For example, the research report included in Appendix E. could be mapped using an inverted funnel as the visual representation of how it is organized. Using the model paper on Planned Parenthood included in Appendix A (APA version) or Appendix B (MLA version) construct a visual map of how that paper is organized. Use another page to draw your representation. To help you get started, begin by outlining the main points of the paper on the remainder of this page. You can then use that outline to help construct your visual map.

Your Name: _____   Date _____

Chapter 4 Exercise 1

There are a total of ten citation errors in the following list of Works Cited. None of the errors are spelling, grammatical or spacing. Circle each error in the following list and provide a correction. Turn the corrected list of Works Cited in to your professor as instructed.

Works Cited

Aldinger, C. "Pentagon Justifies Attack." ABC News.com. 1 Sept. 1999.

    <http://www.abcnews.go.com/go/sections/world/DailyNews/kosovo_

    main_990515.html>.

Bourhis, John. <jsb806f@mail.smsu.edu> Updating the Style Manual. Personal

    email. 1 June 1999. Sept. 29, 1999.

"Call It Cybernoia." Philadelphia Daily News, March 1, 1997, p. 11.

Harnack, Andrew, and Kleppinger, Eugene. Online! A Reference Guide to

    Using Internet Sources. New York: St. Martin's.

Johannesen, R. Ethics in Human Communication, 4th ed. Prospect Heights:

    Waveland Press, 1996.

Nichols, M. The Lost Art of Listening. Prentice-Hall, 1995.

Raymond, Kelly. Toward a New Tolerance: Gun Control and Community

    Policing. Vital Speeches 60 (1993): 332-334.

Wolvin, Andrew, and Carolyn Coakley. Listening, 6th ed. Dubuque: Brown and

    Benchmark, 1995. 223-396.

Your Name: _____   Date _____

Chapter 4 Exercise 2

Based on the information presented in Chapter 1, answer the following questions by writing the best answer in the space provided. For each question, write "T" for true or "F" for false.

_____ 1. <u>MLA</u> stands for Modern Linguistic Association.

_____ 2. <u>MLA</u> style requires that you include a formal title page for every paper you submit for evaluation.

_____ 3. When using a direct quotation, <u>MLA</u> requires that you provide the reader with a page reference for locating the material quoted.

_____ 4. You should seriously consider justifying the right margin of your manuscript because it makes the manuscript look more professional.

_____ 5. It is generally a good idea to keep a Xerox copy of any written work you submit for evaluation for your personal files.

_____ 6. <u>MLA</u> style requires that you always double-space.

_____ 7. Proper pagination in <u>MLA</u> consists of your last name and the page number in the upper right hand corner of the paper.

_____ 8. All scholarly writing submitted for evaluation requires pagination.

_____ 9. The first page of a <u>MLA</u> manuscript is the first page on which the text of the manuscript appears.

_____ 10. In <u>MLA</u>, the list of works cited appears at the end of the paper.

Your Name: _____   Date _____

Chapter 5 Exercise 1

There are at least ten errors in the following list of references. Circle each error in the following list and provide a correction. Turn the corrected list of references in to your instructor.

REFERENCES

Adams, C. A. (1991). Influences on the production and evaluation of regulative messages: Effects of social cognition, situational, and experiential variables in communication between hospital supervisors and volunteers. Unpublished doctoral dissertation: University of Kansas.

Applegate, J. L. (1990). Constructs and communication: A pragmatic integration. In R. Neimeyer & G. Neimeyer (eds.), Advances in personal construct psychology, Vol. 1 (pp. 197-224). Greenwich, CT: JAI.

Applegate, J. L., Burke, J. A., Burleson, B. R., Delia, J.G., and Kline, S. L. (1985). Reflection-enhancing parental communication. In I. E. Siegel (Ed.), Personal belief systems: The psychological consequences for children (pp. 107-142). Hillsdale, NJ: Erlbaum.

Bingham, S. G., & Burleson, B. R. (1988). Multiple effects of messages with multiple goals. Human Communication Research, 16, pp.184-216.

Bonhoeffer, D. (1954). Life Together (J.W. Doberstein, Trans.). San Francisco: Harper San Francisco.

Burgoon, M. (1995). A Kinder, Gentler Discipline: Feeling Good About Being Mediocre. In B. Burelson (Ed.), Communication yearbook 18 (pp. 464-479). Thousand Oaks, CA: Sage.

Burleson, B.R. (1989). The constructivist approach to person-centered communication: Analysis of a research exemplar. In Dervin, B, Grossberg, L, O'Keefe, B. & Wartellam E. (Eds.), Rethinking Communication: Vol. 2. Paradigm Exemplars (pp. 29-46). Newbury Park, CA: Sage.

Cheney, G. (1995). Democracy in the workplace: Theory and practice from the perspective of communication. Journal of Applied Communication Research, 23, 167-200.

Your Name: _____   Date _____

Chapter 5 Exercise 2

The following pages from a sample paper contain at least ten errors in <u>APA</u>
style. Circle each error and provide a correction. Turn the corrected pages in to
your professor as instructed.

Running Head: Supervising Volunteers

SUPERVISING VOLUNTEERS:

INFLUENCES ON THE LOGIC OF MESSAGES DESIGNED TO REGULATE BEHAVIOR

Carey Adams

Southwest Missouri State University

Gregory J. Shepherd

University of Kansas

Supervising Volunteers:

Influences on the Logic of Messages Designed to Regulate Behavior

Volunteerism is an important facet of American society. From de Tocqueville's praise of the volunteer spirit of 19th century America to George Bush's "thousand points of light," volunteerism has been recognized as a virtue in American culture and has been repeatedly called upon in the service of individual and social needs. A recent survey estimated that 80 million American adults donated 19.5 billion hours of service through volunteer efforts in a single year (Ilsley, 1990). Hospitals have traditionally been among the institutions that rely most heavily upon the services of volunteers. Indeed, recent cuts in federal funding have forced social services to rely more heavily on volunteer efforts than ever before (Rosentraub), and hospitals have been steadily expanding their volunteer programs to extend volunteer responsibilities beyond distributing magazines, delivering flowers, and visiting patients (see, for example, the model programs detailed in Developing an older volunteer program, 1981).

The increasing demand for volunteer services in hospitals has led to concern about the retention of volunteer staff in such organizations. A growing body of research has examined questions of volunteer satisfaction (e.g., Paradis, 1987, Lee & Burden, 1990). Not surprisingly, Mausner has shown that the quality of a volunteer's experience is closely related to the quality of the relationship that volunteer enjoys with the supervisory staff of the organization (1988). And, given the wealth of research that has suggested the quality of communication in superior-subordinate relationships is a good predictor of job satisfaction generally (Downs & Hazen, 1976; Pincus, 1986;Clampitt & Downs, 1987; Clampitt & Girardi, 1987), it is not . . ..

INDEX